Just Keep Talking

The Story of the Chat Show

STEVE WRIGHT
with PETER COMPTON

SIMON & SCHUSTER
A VIACOM COMPANY

First published in Great Britain by Simon & Schuster Ltd, 1997
A Viacom Company

Simon & Schuster Ltd
West Garden Place
Kendal Street
London W2 2AQ

Simon & Schuster Australia
Sydney

A CIP catalogue record for this book is available
from the British Library

ISBN 0-684-81699-7

Typeset in Meridien 11/14pt by
Palimpsest Book Production Limited, Polmont, Stirlingshire
Printed and bound in Great Britain by
Butler & Tanner Ltd, Frome and London

CONTENTS

INTRODUCTION

It doesn't matter what you say you just have to look pleased to be there.

Quentin Crisp

Chat – talk in a light familiar way.

Concise Oxford Dictionary

What do Emu, Grace Jones and George Best have in common? Ask any person of a certain age and they will instantly see the connection. Michael Parkinson, Russell Harty and Terry Wogan hosted chat shows for a combined total of almost forty years, interviewing thousands of guests – the good, the bad and the ugly from the worlds of literature, film, sport, music and from right across the social spectrum.

Michael Parkinson considers, quite rightly, that his interview with Professor Jacob Bronowski counts as one of the best seen on television. The eminent man, famous for his TV series *The Ascent of Man*, expounded in layman's terms his philosophy of life. His chilling recollections of his trip to Auschwitz to film part of the series gripped all who saw the interview. When the BBC, in the summer of 1995, showed highlights from the 361-show series the Bronowski interview was omitted. Parkinson told the *Radio Times*, 'The executive producer said, "Are you really suggesting

1 ◆

it's the kind of programme we should put out on primetime on BBC1?" Perhaps not. Not nowadays. Twenty years ago we did. But that is another story altogether.'

Parkinson interviewed well over a thousand guests during his Saturday night tenure but how many specific interviews can you remember? Muhammad Ali, yes, but that's because the host stood up to the boxing heavyweight champion of the world and his forthright views, and came close to being on the receiving end of those famous fists. Who else? It boils down to Emu. Not Rod Hull, his creator, the man in a safari suit with his hand firmly rammed up the antipodean bird's backside. A tatty ventriloquist's dummy upstaged all that had gone before in *Parkinson* history. In twenty seconds of madness the immaculately coiffed host was unceremoniously tipped over in his chair and left sprawling on the floor. Parky kept a smile on his face throughout but it was obvious he was not a happy man.

This was another interview not shown in the 1995 repeat season. He summed up the affair succinctly: 'It tells us a lot about the nature of TV fame. No matter how much we who labour in television might believe that we are enabling nation to speak unto nation, and that it has significance beyond the moment, we should heed the lesson that, after a decade of interviewing the great and the good, all anyone remembers about the *Parkinson* show is that the host was once savaged by a man with a fake bird on his arm.'

Russell Harty, a former teacher, university lecturer and radio arts producer, followed a glittering career path into the chat-show hot-seat. The Blackburn man had won the US television equivalent of an Oscar, an Emmy award, for his stunning documentary on the surrealist artist Salvador Dali. His run of chat shows was even longer than Michael Parkinson's, enriched by an enormous array of guests over the years. But his nemesis arrived in the shape of an Amazonian model-turned-singer, Grace Jones, who like Rod Hull and his Emu have seemingly faded from the public eye. The image of the camp, adenoidal northerner protecting himself from the barrage of left and right hooks from Ms Jones, as she complained that he had turned his back on her, is one of TV's great moments. Harty, who died in 1988, lived under the shadow of that incident for the rest of his life. He often joked that his obituary would read: 'Grace Jones Man Dead'. He wasn't far wrong. The obituaries in the quality press nearly all kicked off with reference to that particular show. Attending a Gracie Fields memorial service at Blackburn cathedral, Harty and Parkinson made a pact: 'If I do yours, will you do mine. You can tell them about Grace Jones and I'll tell them about Emu.'

Terry Wogan ran for over seven years with his shows and clocked up over three thousand guests. With his three-shows-a-week formula running from 1985 it is not surprising that no particular guest stamped their mark on its history: it always seemed to be Howard Keel or that woman who played Dot Cotton in *EastEnders*. Wogan is luckier than his predecessors, however. Yes, George Best was hideously drunk on the show and the host should have been protected by his production team who, at the last minute, might have prevented the shambolic affair. Any other host would have abandoned the interview at birth but the good-hearted Wogan struggled on with polite questions against a mounting tide of gibberish from the former footballing genius. It made every front page the next day but has never been shown again, unlike Emu and Jones. You had to be there to witness that one and the Baron of Blarney is probably more than grateful that it is unlikely to grace the airwaves again.

The journalist Mark Steyn summed up the British experience in 1993 as *Aspel & Co.* was on its last legs: 'In Britain we have the chat but not the "show". Close your eyes and visualize the Aspel show. What is it? A weedy signature tune you can't quite recall, an anonymous set, a couple of uncomfortable looking chairs.'

Oh! Of course there's David Frost (Didn't he have a run-in with that crooked insurance man Savundra?); Eamonn Andrews (Wasn't he Britain's first true chat host in 1964 and made headlines in the paper after almost every show because of the behaviour of his guests?); what about that Michael Aspel (He had a very, very drunk Oliver Reed on his show didn't he?); and Simon Dee (Well he did interview lots of people but his fame grew with his many run-ins with his TV bosses).

So that's the chat show, in Britain at least. It would be easy to encapsulate the genre in an essay. Who needs a book? No one could possibly remember individual shows. Only the hosts' careers remain. However the story of how the chat show evolved from its early beginnings in New York at the birth of television to today's anarchic 'gabfests' is a fascinating one. The British chat show has never been subjected to a history before and the authors are mindful that the majority of US shows are largely unseen here except for the minority with cable and satellite. Johnny Carson, former host of the *Tonight Show*, is probably one of the most famous men in the US but remains a virtual unknown here along with Jay Leno and David Letterman. David Frost is the only man in the field who has clicked with both countries.

Today the chat show is omnipresent. It may be reasonably sparse on terrestrial television (usurped perhaps by the daytime talk show) but both cable and satellite have unlocked the genre. Many viewers in this country can experience not only the best that America has to offer but also the third-rate shows which many British programmers would never consider buying. It's now possible to watch each night the *Tonight Show* and the *Late Show* just one day after US transmission and sample the flavour of what's making news in that country. Granada has recently launched a channel, Granada Talk, which is devoted to such shows. The global village, a much talked about entity in the 1960s, is now firmly established. Talk, talk and more talk has been the standard for many years in the US and now Britain seems ready to absorb even more of that culture.

HISTORY

These shows are about the guy behind the desk.
                                        Johnny Carson

The chat show was born on US television on 29 May 1950, when *Broadway Open House* aired for the first time on the NBC network. The concept was simplicity itself. When actors, actresses and variety stars finished their performance on The Great White Way they informally dropped into the TV studios to entertain or merely chat. This was all backed up with a team of regulars who performed sketches, songs and dances. The idea had been dreamed up by NBC network executive Sylvester L. 'Pat' Weaver, Jr to fill the 11 p.m. slot Monday through Friday. Comedian Don 'Creesh' Hornsby had been selected to become the first host but tragically he was given a diagnosis of polio on the day he was to sign his contract and died two weeks later. Two veteran comedians, Jerry Lester and Morey Amsterdam, took over, sharing host duties (Amsterdam later became a famous name in Britain when he appeared in the *Dick Van Dyke Show* as Buddy Sorrell).

A major problem for NBC was to find an audience at such a late hour to fill their studio. Amsterdam found a simple solution in contacting tourist bus companies and asking them to recommend a trip to a TV show alongside their customer's regular jaunts to nightclubs and the theatre. The show ran fifteen months with an ever-changing cast amongst which was Dagmar, a statuesque dumb blonde hired by Jerry Lester to read poetry in a deadpan style. She soon became a star of the show and Lester began to resent her (even introducing another blonde, Agathon) to the extent that he quit the series which then quickly folded. *Broadway Open House* was a major success, not least because at its time slot opposition was almost non-existent. It proved there was an audience for chat, interspersed with performances, but the genre lay moribund for almost two years until a certain Steve Allen began his own show for WNBC in Manhattan in 1953.

Allen was a true original and is generally considered the founding father of the chat show as we now know it. He arrived in New York in 1950 to act as host on a variety of game and quiz shows before landing the *Steve Allen Show*. It was such a success locally that NBC decided to make it a network show. It was renamed *Tonight* and made its debut on 27 September 1954. Like *Broadway Open House* it relied on talent from the theatre and club world and promised that Allen would act 'as stagedoor Johnny for millions of viewers'. *Tonight* was an instant success with Allen's frenetic style to the fore. The show was the blueprint for everything that followed.

Allen appeared at the beginning, delivered a monologue and then sat behind his desk and his guests sat next to him on a couch. Celebrities queued up to appear as the show became a vital platform to plug a new book, film or TV show. The audience was an integral part of the action, participating in games such as Stump the Band, a quiz that remained a staple of *Tonight* history. The show ventured out of the theatre, into the street where Allen would be a hot dog vendor or simply conduct interviews with passers by. Actor Tony Randall was tracked down Broadway as he raced to the studio after a show to be interviewed, a camera following his every perilous step as he sprinted through the crowds. Guests didn't have to be celebrities: inventors, people with unusual talents or pets were all worthy subjects for an Allen interview. The host's crowning moment was when the show was being broadcast from Miami one week and he persuaded a platoon of US Marines to stage a mock invasion on the beach. Many tourists in the area were led into a blind panic thinking the US Eastern seaboard was under attack by foreign invaders.

Allen hosted his last show on 25 January 1957, switching to the Sunday night *Steve Allen Show* which went out head-to-head with the *Ed Sullivan Show*. Chat shows began to proliferate mainly because of the immense amount of money they generated against minimal costs. Allen had been paid the relatively large sum of $3,500 a week during his tenure but the guests appeared on a union scale of just $265.50 per show. A 90-minute show, five days a week, generated a phenomenal advertising revenue for TV stations.

With Allen's departure the chat show collapsed into the doldrums with the replacement show *Tonight! America After Dark*. The format was much like breakfast television today, perhaps with the caveat, 'a mission to inform'. There were still interviews with the famous and trips out to Broadway but this was underlined with more serious fare such as visits to hospitals and planetariums. News and politics were a vital part of the mix with live link-ups between New York, Chicago and Los Angeles. The show was a complete flop: America wanted to be entertained, not educated, at bedtime and NBC scrapped the show in July 1957.

It seemed that the genius of Steve Allen would be irreplaceable but another game-show host was waiting in the wings in the shape of Jack Paar who would stamp his authority on the format. Three days after the final broadcast of *Tonight! America After Dark*, the *Jack Paar Show* took over the late-night slot for NBC. Parr used the opposite of Allen's agitated style, appearing as a relaxed host adept at interviewing and becoming personally involved with his guests. His opening monologues were delivered haphazardly but endearingly, typical subjects being a trip to the dentists that day or a birthday party for one of his children. His sheer normality struck a chord with the average viewer. It was not unusual to see him crying at a poignant story or becoming so angry about something on air he would announce he was quitting the show and walk off the set. America lapped it up.

He promoted Fidel Castro on air and lambasted the Batista regime in Cuba, he interviewed both Nixon and Kennedy in election year 1960 and some shows were broadcast from the Berlin Wall. He had a knack of drawing out naturally reserved guests. Judy Garland was a case in point: a dynamic singer but not relaxed in conversational mode. Paar conjured out her chatty side and she became an audience favourite with her stories about Hollywood.

The personal angst of the host on live television proved too much, however, for the network, who instigated a policy of taping the show early evening to avoid any controversy. This led to Paar's departure in February 1960 after NBC removed one of his jokes about a water-closet. He stayed on the sidelines for a month before rejoining the show but the rift between star and network proved deep and he quit in March 1962 (breaking down in tears throughout the final show).

Once more a game-show host filled the void in the shape of Johnny Carson but he was committed to hosting the quiz show *Who Do You Trust?* until October 1962. NBC decided to carry on with the *Tonight Show* using a succession of guest hosts, including Groucho Marx, Merv Griffin, Jerry Lewis and Donald O'Connor. Carson finally took the host's seat on 2 October 1962 and remained there for over 30 years, becoming part of the fabric of the American way of life.

Born in Corning, Iowa, Carson was the epitome of the Midwest and almost the opposite of the emotionally transparent Paar. His cool, reserved style acted as a perfect filter for his guests and his background in stand-up comedy allowed him to fire back quips at will. He could ride the show through any amount of foul-ups with a studied wisecrack, exhibiting a Zen-like calm throughout.

With sidekick Ed McMahon acting as a durable foil at the end of the sofa Carson became known as the 'man who has logged more hours in our bedrooms than many a lover'.

At the end of a long working day American citizens could retire to their bedrooms safe in the knowledge that after their dose of Carson all was right in the world. His monologues utilized the best comic writing talent available and his laconic style made the delivery pitch perfect. Comic sketches introduced audiences to a wide range of characters that included bumbling magician Carnac the Magnificent, Carswell the mind-reader and all-American patriot Floyd R. Turbo. The Mighty Carson Art Players provided regular spoofs of news events, films and TV shows. The marriage of Tiny Tim to Miss Vicki on the show (17 December 1969) sent viewing figures through the roof.

The show switched from New York to Los Angeles in 1972, opening up a wider vista of guests from Hollywood. Carson saw off challenges from many other rivals during his tenure, including Alan Thicke, Dennis Miller, Pat Sajak, Merv Griffin, Dick Cavett, Les Crane, Joey Bishop, David Brenner, Gary Shandling and Joan Rivers. As his salary and NBC's profits rocketed the old guard remained firm throughout every trend which came and went.

When the *Tonight Show* cut back from 90 minutes to one hour in September 1980 Carson gave the go-ahead for another chat show to air directly after his. *Late Night with David Letterman* made its debut on 2 February 1982. Letterman was very much in the mould of Carson: another Midwesterner from Indianapolis who brought a new angle to the chat-show scene.

Broadcasting from New York the show presented an anti-establishment tone firmly rooted in the style of Steve Allen. Cameras were plainly in view along with cue-cards as the host weaved his way around the studio interacting with the audience. Melons were thrown off the top of buildings and filmed in slow motion to witness the effect of hitting the sidewalk, members of the public performed anatomically challenging tricks and a chimpanzee was allowed to roam the set with a camera on his head.

Letterman was the first of a new wave of hosts whose appeal reached an urban audience tired of hackneyed showbiz stars and the strictures of old-time variety-style television. Letterman was totally clued into his guests, with a razor-sharp mind and the ability to pounce on anyone at the first sign of pretention. Guests had to be either very careful or the host's equal in verbal duelling. Letterman's controversial interview with Madonna was a case in point. She managed to stand her ground throughout the show but resorted to swearing to garner credibility. Letterman won the bout hands down with his casual air and assured control, never rising to the bait.

As the eighties gave way to the nineties a host of wannabees appeared aiming for the all-important younger demographic. Arsenio Hall, Whoopi Goldberg, Howard Stern and Vicki Lawrence all fronted hipper versions of the *Tonight Show*. Carson still remained king, however, with the conservative audience who made up the majority of the US viewing public.

In 1991 the unthinkable happened when Carson announced his retirement from showbusiness at the completion of the 1991–92 *Tonight* season. On 22 May 1992 Carson presented his final *Tonight Show* to an invited audience of friends of the cast and crew. His 30-year reign at the top was over. The last programme was a compilation of highlights from the 22,000-plus guests he had interviewed on the famous sofa. David Letterman seemed the odds-on contender to replace Carson but the job went to comedian Jay Leno, a former guest host on the show.

The producers of the show decided to wipe the slate clean in terms of presentation. Out went Carson's house band led by Doc Severinsen and in came the cool jazz of Branford Marsalis. The set was also redesigned. Leno took time to click, but now the show has established itself as a ratings winner Carson's successor has proven himself as a suitable mixture of hip and tradition. He has the verve and cynicism needed to attract the young urban viewer but also retains an old-school aura of the showbusiness from which Carson emanated. This tricky balancing act has allowed the *Tonight Show* to retain the status it has held since 1950.

The chat show in Britain has always owed everything to the US format which has been slavishly followed right up to the present. The first programme which could remotely be called a chat show was *Face to Face* which first aired on the BBC. Journalist John Freeman sat in the shadows with his back to the camera and questioned celebrities with a barrage of questions which demanded quick and lucid answers. By today's standards Freeman's method seems almost akin to a Gestapo grilling. Tony Hancock's reasons for being a comedian were brutally dissected by Freeman forcing Hancock to bare his soul to the nation. Broadcaster Gilbert Harding was reduced to tears when asked if he had ever been in the presence of death as he began to relate the passing of his mother. The sheer starkness of style has never been witnessed again on television and few celebrities today would allow themselves such a rough ride.

It wasn't until the *Eamonn Andrews Show* launched in 1964 that Britain finally caught up with the US. Broadcast late on Sundays, it had a budget sufficient to snag the biggest stars in town, a seasoned but anodyne host at the helm and a selection of guests who were always willing to push against what was then deemed respectable with borderline behaviour and language. David Frost took the US format for the chat show and broadened its horizons extensively. He was so successful he reconfigured the whole formula of the genre and sold it back to America (in much the same way that The Beatles distilled black pop music into an acceptable sound for the mainstream and gave it back to its country of origin).

Frost's most important contribution was to utilize the studio audience in debate, an idea streamlined even more by Phil Donahue in the US that gradually became the standard for all daytime chat shows. Michael Parkinson dominated the 1970s with his *Tonight*-style show which with British humility emblazoned the host's name everywhere but allowed him very modestly to take a back seat to his guests – something which would be unthinkable in the US where the host has much more airtime than his guests.

In the 1980s Terry Wogan was the first (and probably the last) person to host a show in primetime three times a week. From day one he was up against the critics who allowed no room for gradual improvement; every night had to be a major event, but the paucity of top-line guests soon became the show's undoing. Unfortunately, the show had long run out of steam before the decade had ended and the final years were proof positive that Wogan had been wilfully exposed in being allowed to carry on with a show that was stamped 'best before 1990'. Jonathan Ross sparked life into the format with *The Last Resort* for Channel 4, where, like many American shows, the host's comedy antics took precedence over the guests.

In 1997 the chat show in the traditional format is a rarity on British television. We have nothing approaching the *Tonight Show* and major name interviewers have been put out to grass. David Frost appeared briefly on Carlton attempting to revive the *Frost Programme* format but there is little in the dedicated form of host, desk, sofa. *Clive Anderson All Talk* is perhaps the closest to this tradition but the erudite barrister host tackles his guests in a cross-examination style which most often extends to a points scoring exercise rather than a conversation. Britain seems much more at home with the daytime format both homegrown and imported.

In the UK, David Frost is certainly the progenitor of the interactive chat-show format, but Phil Donahue is the man who took the whole concept to extremes, creating the atmosphere of a town or council meeting in the studio with shocking subject matter for debate. The *Phil Donahue Show* began life on WLWD-TV in Dayton, Ohio on 6 November 1967. The first programme featured an atheist called Madalyn Murray O'Hair and before the end of that year guests had included a funeral director (for part of the show Donahue had reclined in a coffin); an admitted homosexual (a revelation for TV at that time); and a debate on a newly launched anatomical doll, correct in every detail. From these humble beginnings the foundations of daytime chat were laid.

Ten years later *Donahue* was the number one syndicated chat show in the US, with subjects ranging from lesbian mothers who have custody of their children to penis enlargements. Oprah Winfrey, Geraldo Rivera and Sally Jessy Raphael all followed in his footsteps, whilst Britain weighed in with the likes of *Kilroy* and *Esther*. Topics for American daytime chat sum up the format: 'Incredible Love Triangle – Man Marries His Mother-In-Law', 'Jell–O Wrestling – Is it Sexist?' and 'Mom, When My Boyfriend Gets Out of Jail I'm Taking Him Back'.

In 1995 the *Jenny Jones Show* instigated a murder. The subject was 'Secret Crushes on People of the Same Sex'. A common formula for daytime shows was revealing secret admirers. In this case a 24-year-old waiter from Lake Orion, Michigan, one John Schmitz, attended a taping in the mistaken belief his secret admirer was a woman. He was devastated when his admirer was revealed as a male bartender, Scott Amedure. When Amedure approached him at his house a few days later, Schmitz snapped and shot the bartender.

In the US in 1996 the ultimate homage to the chat show was paid: a full length TV movie (based on Bill Carter's best-selling book *The Late Shift*) about the battle for ratings between Jay Leno and David Letterman was aired. Leno was played by Daniel Roebuck sporting a monster-sized prosthetic jaw, whilst Letterman was portrayed by John Michael Higgins, a man with red hair. Both hosts were instantly dismissive. Leno told Larry King, 'We just write jokes, you know? I don't quite get what the story is.' Letterman called the film 'the biggest waste of film since my wedding photos' and likened Higgins's portrayal to a 'psychotic chimp'. Leno claimed to be puzzled by the whole thing: 'There couldn't be two duller guys than Dave and I. It's not a book about two hosts banging hookers in the dressing room and doing coke. We both go home at night and work on the act.'

Chat is still the province of both daytime and night-time television in the US but in this country the latter appears to be moribund. Parkinson and Wogan acknowledge that they have had their day but little new talent appears willing to sit behind the host desk and television companies seem reluctant to create a show. The highly talented Gaby Roslin gamely tried on Channel 4 with a no-frills approach but there is no doubt the lack of Grade A guests proved a major setback. After the disastrously reviewed series a spokesperson for Channel 4 proclaimed the talk show was dead in this country. But Gaby will keep trying. She is, after all, the epitome of the girl next door. The repeats of *Parkinson* in 1995 and 1996 have shown exactly how exciting the format can be. It remains to be seen if anyone can take up the mantle in this country.

JOHNNY CARSON

I want my na-na.
Johnny Carson's opening line to the audience
on his 1962 *Tonight Show* Debut

The impact of Johnny Carson and the *Tonight Show* as part of the fabric of the United States is best underlined by his monologue delivered on 19 December 1973. *Tonight Show* writers had picked up on a news report of a paper shortage reported by the Government Printing Office. They corrupted the story so Carson could deliver the line: 'But have you heard the latest? I'm not kidding, I saw it in the paper. There's a shortage of toilet paper.' Within hours America was on the move. Supermarkets from Los Angeles to New York were stripped of toilet paper as people began to horde as much of the stuff as possible. It was only a few days later when news reports could debunk the myth that buying eased up and toilet tissue once more filled the shelves. Such was the power wielded by the comedian from Corning, Iowa.

Although before his retirement in 1992 Carson was probably one of the most recognisable men in America, alongside the President and Elvis Presley, he is virtually unknown in this country. London Weekend Television picked up a package of shows to combat *Parkinson* in 1981 but the viewing levels were in thousands rather than millions. Carson is the solid embodiment of middle America and his mastery of wisecracking and ability to keep a show on course could never find an audience here. When he took over the *Tonight Show* in 1962 America was entertained for 105 minutes from 11.30 p.m. onwards, many watching on their bedroom television set. Contrast this to the Britain of 1962. Programmes were about to end at this time, winding down on ITV with the Epilogue. A second TV was virtually unheard of in a British household and watching in bed would have been akin to decadent behaviour. Although Carson is rightly regarded as the foundation stone of the chat show he is generally disparaged in this country as far too showbiz-based to be of any credibility. This attitude belies the man who refined comedy and the art of communication to new levels.

He served in the navy during World War II in the Pacific on USS *Pennsylvania* and at demob joined the University of Nebraska, where he gained a BA degree. His senior thesis was based on comedy writing where he analyzed the work of screen and radio comedians such as Jack Benny and Bob Hope. He started his broadcasting career at a local radio station in Lincoln, Nebraska, working on a morning serial, *Eddie Sosby and the Radio Rangers*. Local television followed in 1949 as the host of an afternoon show called *The Squirrel's Nest*. He moved to Los Angeles in 1951 to become the host of KNXT-TV providing continuity links and programme introductions. The following year he began his own show, *Carson's Cellar*, which with its offbeat comedy became a favourite with such luminaries as Groucho Marx, Red Skelton, Fred Allen and Jack Benny, who all agreed to appear on the show.

Benny was one of the biggest comedians in America at that time and for a young, untested comic to feature him as a guest on his show was a major achievement. The two became lifelong friends thereafter and Benny became a regular guest on the *Tonight Show*. He graduated to *Carson's Coffee Break* and the quiz show *Earn Your Money*. He also wrote material for Red Skelton's show and when Carson replaced him on air after a studio accident he became an instant hit with viewers. It led to the *Johnny Carson Show* which ran through a succession of writers and directors who tried in vain to alter his natural style to something more like the then hot TV favourite Jackie Gleason. Although it ran for 39 weeks it was Carson's first failure. Another format of the *Johnny Carson Show* was aired as a daytime item but this too flopped. He moved to New York in 1956 concentrating on his stand-up comedy and soon landed the host job on the TV game show *Do You Trust Your Wife?* (later renamed *Who Do You Trust?*).

In 1958 Carson made his Broadway debut replacing Tom Ewell in the comedy *Tunnel of Love*. He later turned down the lead in the hit musical *Bye Bye Birdie* because of commitment to his TV show. He acted as a replacement for Jack Paar on the *Tonight Show* during this period and discovered he enjoyed and was adept in the role of chat-show host. When Paar decided to quit in March 1962 Carson was the natural successor and NBC were prepared to wait until his *Who Do You Trust?* contract expired in September of that year to get their man. At a time when most comedians thrived on their ethnic background, Carson seemed destined, with his boyish good looks and neat style, to be warmly accepted by audiences across America as they prepared for sleep.

On 1 October 1962, at NBC's Studio 6B in New York, Groucho Marx introduced the new host of the *Tonight Show* to an expectant America. Carson told the audience, 'Jack Paar was king of late-night television. Why don't you just consider me the prince?' The debut line-up was Mel Brooks, Joan Crawford, Rudy Vallee and Tony Bennett. He was an immediate smash hit, his ratings rapidly overtaking Jack Paar's performance. The show became so popular, with an average nightly audience of ten million viewers, that Carson could dictate salary terms with NBC. His salary leapt from $200,000 to $390,000 by 1964. Carson developed his own style from the beginning, filling the show with items such as spinning hula hoops with Miss USA or indulging in a wrestling bout with a professional. He continually honed his comedic craft and became a master of blurring the boundary between normality and outrageousness.

In 1964 Carson instigated the first of many comic characters who would become synonymous with the show. Carnac the Magnificent was a turbaned mystic who could provide answers to questions contained in a white envelope pressed to his forehead. The answer would be announced followed by the question. For example, Answer: 'The coal-miner's daughter'; Question: 'Where can you pick up a nasty soot-rash?' Or, Answer: 'A linen closet'; Question: 'What do gay Irish guys come out of?' The most popular Carnac Answer was 'Sis boom bah', in answer to the Question: 'Describe the sound of a sheep blowing up?'

Other characters included Aunt Blabby, a feisty OAP, disastrous magician El Moldo, super-patriot Floyd R. Turbo and movie pitchman Art Fern. In 1966 the Mighty Carson Art Players were formed, an ever-changing repertory group who provided topical sketches. Singer Jimmy Dean was the first guest host, in 1963, his comedy stand-up act featuring in later shows. By 1992, 124 different guests had hosted the show.

Carson walked from the show in April 1967 when NBC aired old shows (he rightly felt that his jokes from these transmissions were no longer topical) and Dean took over to a less than enthusiastic viewership. The ratings fell through the floor and Carson was welcomed back with open arms and a salary to match; over $4 million (from $7,500 a week to $20,000) to take him up to 1970. The show was also shortened by fifteen minutes to an hour and a half.

ABC launched the first of many *Tonight Show* competitors that year when former *Tonight* guest host Joey Bishop appeared with a late-night chat show. Launched during Carson's walk-out it had an inauspicious beginning when Ronald Reagan was fourteen minutes late on the premiere night. On night two, guest Buddy Greco was introduced, the curtain went back and revealed an empty stage. Greco was still in his dressing room. After these beginnings the show never really got off the starting blocks, competing with the publicity generated by Carson's departure and his later triumphal return. Another late-night rival, Merv

Griffin, was launched in 1969 by CBS. His show lasted until 1972, killed off the *Joey Bishop Show* (replaced by Dick Cavett), but never achieved its aim to be a serious rival to Carson. Dick Cavett brought thought-provoking conversation and guests to late night but his show was disposed of in 1972 as Carson continued to reign triumphantly.

It took almost another ten years before another attempt was made to scale the mighty Carson castle. Canadian Alan Thicke hosted the syndicated show *Thicke of the Night*. Attempting to be hip and attracting a young audience with rock songs and young comics it was a complete flop, despite major publicity. In 1989 young black comedian and actor Arsenio Hall succeeded in building up a core audience in syndication of young urban blacks. CBS tried again with the *Pat Sajak Show* but its formality and conservative style was at odds with a younger audience and was consigned to the dumper a year later. Ronald Reagan (son of the ex-president) and *Saturday Night Live* comedian Dennis Miller both tried and failed to make a dent on the *Tonight Show*. Carson remained the king throughout.

> *It was a great moment. A great moment personally and for TV history. It was satellited all over the world. It was written up in three encyclopedias.*
> Tiny Tim on his wedding on the *Tonight Show*

The *Tonight Show* on 17 December 1969 saw one of its biggest-ever audiences when man-child singer Tiny Tim married Miss Vicki live on air in front of 45 million viewers. This equalled almost an 85% share of the American public tuned in that night. The late Tiny Tim was a plump, long-haired falsetto singer something in the mould of an American George Formby. His main claim to fame was to play his ukulele whilst screeching out a version of 'Tiptoe Through the Roses'. This along with a repertoire of songs from the twenties and thirties was his act. No one could explain why his televised wedding became such an event. What made the show was Carson playing along in his inimitable straight-man role. Not once did he show any sign of mirth at the bizarre proceedings unfolding before the audience. Tiny Tim toasted his new bride with milk and honey and then sang two songs, the 'Wedding Song For Miss Vicki' and 'You Were There'. Outside of Royal weddings it was probably the most witnessed wedding in the world ever (the couple divorced in 1977).

To any American of a certain age the most memorable Carson moment occurred in 1965 with Ed Ames and his tomahawk act. Ames was a co-star in the TV series *Daniel Boone* in the role of Mingo, a red indian. Demonstrating his tomahawk hurling skills at a wooden cut-out of a man his first throw landed squarely in the crotch. Carson instantly quipped, 'I didn't even know you were Jewish', before erupting with the audience into three minutes and 25 seconds of uninterrupted laughter. As the wails of the audience subsided Ames asked Carson, 'Johnny, do you want to try it?' to which he replied, 'Why? You can't hurt a fella worse.' This clip became one of the most famous moments on the *Tonight Show* thanks to its constant repeats on anniversary shows. It even inspired a sketch on *Saturday Night Live* when Dan Aykroyd attacked a cut-out with an axe until nothing was left.

> *Heeeeere's Johnny . . .*
> Jack Nicholson in *The Shining*

An integral part of the *Tonight Show* was Carson's monologue at the beginning of the show, where the dapper host, often resplendent in a tuxedo, stepped out from behind a shimmering curtain and returned to his roots in stand-up (assisted, however, by material from the cream of US comedy writers). The seven-minute spiel, based on what was happening in America, grabbed the nation's attention like nothing else on television. Pundits claimed that the monologue was more avidly absorbed than any news bulletin or presidential address. When Americans switched off their bedroom light they could sleep sound in the knowledge that President Johnny was watching over them. Indeed many Americans just needed their monologue fix and were soundly asleep before any guests appeared.

Yes, Carson had the best writers money could afford but his delivery was unique. He had the ability to ride out any gags that fell flat purely by his demeanour or a well chosen ad lib. Instead of cue-cards read chronologically his whole speech was laid out in a long line so he could switch instantly to another area if a subject was not reacting with the audience. His writers never knew until showtime which gags would be used. The day's quota was delivered to Carson a few hours before taping and he would trim down the material that he felt would work. His apprenticeship as a comedian also stood him in good stead during a writer's strike when he delivered his own material seamlessly. The monologue always ended with the legendary Carson golf-swing, the precursor to the next part of the show.

Journalist John Lofflin outlined what Carson, and especially his opening spiel, meant to America: 'His sense of wonder is also important to the sense of the world we collectively share as a society. Who has not experienced some awful trauma – the death of a parent, a divorce, a lost job – and not turned to Carson for healing? He is, in an odd sense, the poor man's analyst. He doesn't listen and he doesn't offer advice, but he is solace and he is always there. The world will go on, he says with his presence, with his natty suit and his Nebraska smile. The heart might be breaking, but Carson's warm glow persists, promises a night of unchallenging entertainment (even if one is too distraught to pay attention) and promises to return tomorrow.'

Carson's other art is the zinger, the instant quip that is fired off effortlessly without recourse to a script. When golfer Arnold Palmer appeared on the show Carson asked him if his wife did anything to wish him luck before his tournaments. Palmer: 'She washes my balls'; Carson: 'I guess that makes your putter stand up.' A female pretzel baker demonstrated her art on the show, looping long strands of dough. Carson couldn't do it. 'Here try this piece, I don't think yours is long enough,' said the baker. Carson fired back, 'Yes, I think I've heard that one before.' Demonstrating a magic trick to a four-year-old spelling champion, Rohan Varavadekar, Carson made the coin vanish from his hand and produced it from the boy's ear. 'How did you make it disappear,' asked Rohan. 'Simple,' said the host, 'You get married.' Guest Denise Wells explained how she had been arrested at a George Strait concert after using the men's toilets because of a large queue at the ladies. The police cautioned her that she had behaved 'in a manner likely to cause a disturbance'. She told them the trip was a necessity and she wasn't window-shopping, to which Carson replied, 'I think the correct term is comparison shopping.'

When the audience gave him an unending ovation one night, he stepped in front of the curtain and quipped, 'Thank you, look I, c'mon folks, sorry but I was warned never to take applause from strangers. But be honest, after two hours in line you would applaud a box of stale wheat thins.' When Zsa Zsa Gabor appeared with a Persian cat on her lap she asked, 'Johnny would you like to pet my pussy?' He replied, 'Sure, if you move the damn cat out of the way.'

What made you a star? – Audience member
I started out in a gaseous state. Then I cooled. – Johnny Carson

Journalist Neil Shister defined Carson's art in the book *Here's Johnny* by Stephen Cox. He notes that Carson was famed for a surly attitude off screen and an almost fanatical desire to keep his private life just that. 'What Carson does is puncture bunkum with deadpan humour of polished economy, in a moment of upward-rolling eyeballs or a startled shake of his head as if he were dozing off, he expresses stunned disbelief or disagreement. This is his nightly genius, this talent for building a laugh off an unwitting straight man seated on his right, while still maintaining the façade of the dutiful host displaying his best manners. He makes conversation on camera the way, say, Picasso might have doodled: less an end in itself than a prelude to something grander. In Carson's case, that means a topper, a joke spontaneously pulled out of the air that suddenly gives order to an unstructured dialogue. One doesn't watch Carson to hear what others have to say (too often they tend to be show-biz glitter types of the most passing interest) but rather to watch Carson work.'

Famed US psychiatrist Dr Joyce Brothers has another take on Carson's undying popularity: 'It's because we know so little about him. He's familiar, but at the same time you don't know much about his personal life, so you can project onto him what you want him to be. He can be your cute son, the dad you wish you had, your lover, the man who got away, your best buddy. Johnny has made himself famous into a Rorschach for America.'

Author Erica Jong speculated: 'What must it be like to have to be publicly brilliant night after night? People turn on the tube half asleep and Johnny's is the last face they see before oblivion hits. He became part of their dreams. And dreams often determine the rest of their lives. What a responsibility and what a burden. I try to imagine what it would be like to be Johnny Carson. I imagine waking up in the morning, knowing that at five in the afternoon I would have to make the entire country laugh. It's not in the nature of human beings to be consistently, predictably funny. So the man who served as America's court jester for three decades sometimes had to rely on a special intimacy with his loyal audience to get through bad nights. But the face of the jester, with its familiar dimples, its thatch of silvering hair, was always a comforting presence before the arms of Morpheus claimed us.'

In 1972 the whole show moved from New York to Los Angeles, on the doorstep of Hollywood, endeavouring to attract more stars at the heart of the film industry. NBC built a new complex at their Burbank studio to accommodate the *Tonight Show*. But Carson's rapport with his audience – 'one of them' – was never broken, he never appeared to have 'gone Hollywood'. The man from the heartland of America was hip but he never lost his Midwestern roots. Fellow chat-show host Dick Cavett defined Carson thus: 'There's a sense of danger. You don't know what he might say next. He's got that fraternity emcee, bad boy quality with the Midwestern overlay that makes him acceptable to audiences. He's got a touch of Huck Finn, a touch of Groucho and more than a touch of Benny and Hope.'

> *Johnny Carson has done more to ruin America's love life*
> *than anyone else in the country. On any given night that*
> *he's hosting the* Tonight Show *there are ten times more*
> *couples watching his monologue than making love.*
>   Dr Ruth Westheimer

Another constant on the show was Ed McMahon, the man for whom the phrase 'second banana' fitted like that fruit's skin. They met professionally in 1957 when McMahon won the job as prize announcer on Carson's quiz show *Who Do You Trust?*. They teamed up once more at the very beginning of Carson's tenure on the *Tonight Show*. McMahon defined his role in 1971: 'I'm also companion, assistant, consultant, and devil's advocate.' He was permanently stationed at the end of the sofa where Carson could bounce off gags and questions if his star guests were not responsive. During the monologue McMahon's 'ho-ho-ho's' (off camera) where a vital foil for Carson's jokes. Most importantly he was the man each night who announced, 'Here's Johnny'. McMahon remained a constant on the show from the beginning to the end. The third element in the team was band leader, Carl 'Doc' Severinsen. Skitch Henderson had fronted the band through the Allen and Paar years and stayed with Carson until Milton DeLugg took over. Severensen, a long-term musician on the show, took over as band leader in 1967. His jazzy trumpet was a perfect foil to the cool Carson lounge style. Stump the Band was an integral part of the show as audience members challenged Severensen and co to play requests.

Television is an intimate medium. I'm not conscious when I use the camera. I know it's there. I use it like another person and do a reaction at it – lift an eyebrow or shrug or whatever.

Johnny Carson

An essential part of the show was the appearance of members of the public who could perform strange feats or had odd interests. Known as 'civilians' by the production team they became a mainstay of the programme. Carson had the knack of making the most nervous guest feel at home. He told *Rolling Stone* magazine in 1979, 'I like to work with elderly people and children. I don't know why. Maybe it's the vulnerability of them. There's a charm about older people that sometimes is childlike, and I enjoy them because, first of all, they can say anything they want to, which is just great. Age gives you a leg up on what you can say, because you don't have to account to anybody. You've lived your life and earned the right to sound off. They'll say, "Oh, well screw that, I don't like that, that's a lot of shit", and they lay it right out.'

Civilian guests ranged from ladies over the age of 100, to a man who made jewellery from quail droppings, to potato crisp collector, Myrtle Young. Young became a star on the show with her unique ability to spot crisps that sported the outline of such things as a bird, dog or even cartoon character Yogi Bear. She was employed on the production line at a crisp factory so had plenty of time to indulge in her hobby. Carson perpetrated a cruel gag on her when she was distracted by switching her treasured collection for regular crisps and hastily munching on them.

Johnny Carson would make a fine president.

Douglas Warde Kelley

Another mainstay of the show was the appearance of wild animals from zoos. A constant parade, ranging from elephants to spiders kept audiences delighted, in no small part due to Carson's natural affinity with the creatures. Perky monkeys, talking parrots and a marmoset who staked out his territory on Carson's head all helped to keep a perfect balance with the star guests. The animal stars were never rushed to perform and quite often a star guest could be bumped off that night's show if the animal proved to be an entertaining item.

Guests of the human kind were subtly kept in check by the host. Journalist John Lofflin analyzed Carsons behaviour with guests: 'While Johnny has always been the perfect host, his guests have not always shared that mission. Many have seemed all too eager to shock, allowing black lace dresses to ride up nearly to their chins – or so it seemed – or holding forth with a series of words that would almost certainly be bleeped from rebroadcast. More often than not, the on-the-air Johnny Carson was not pleased, and he showed it, in gentle, subtle ways. Rarely has he been offensive in our homes, rarely has he insulted his guests, pushed them to reveal more than they wanted, milked their misfortunes for sensation.'

> *Who's the man that we admire. Johnny Carson is a real live wire.*
> 'Johnny Carson' by the Beach Boys

By 1980 the show was trimmed to just one hour a night with the host contracted to appear four nights a week. He was paid over $5 million a year and became producer/owner of the show. He was also allowed to set up his own television projects, one of which was *Late Night with David Letterman*. The year 1986 saw one of TV's most famous feuds erupt when the fledgeling Fox network announced that Joan Rivers would be hosting her own chat show at 10 p.m. each weekday night in an attempt to woo viewers away from Carson.

The rancour evolved because Rivers was a regular guest anchor on the *Tonight Show* and Carson only learnt the news of defection like everyone else when Fox issued their press release. Carson had given the comedienne her showbusiness break on the show in 1965 when he literally wept with laughter at her routine and told America she was going to be a star. She became a regular on the show and by 1983 had become the permanent guest host on *Tonight*. When she defected Carson never spoke to her again. Her show was a failure, her three-year contract was curtailed by Fox but later she bounced back with a daytime talk show and appearances on the QVC shopping channel.

A 1987 deal saw Carson's salary increase to $10 million a year with fifteen weeks of holiday and just three nights a week in the host's chair. One of the most memorable interviews on the show took place on 6th May 1991. Michael Landon, long-time US TV star of *Bonanza*, *The Little House on the Prairie* and *Highway to Heaven* had less than two months to live after being diagnosed with pancreatic and liver cancer. He bravely agreed to appear on the show to dispel rumours of his condition and indulged in repartee with his long-time friend Carson. He was determined to show up the US trash tabloids who had created many stories, mostly untrue, about his condition. It was his last public appearance and attracted an audience second only to the Tiny Tim wedding ceremony. Landon died on 1st July 1991.

> *I'm one of the lucky people in the world. I found something I've always wanted to do and I've enjoyed every single minute of it. I bid you a very heartfelt good night.*
>   Johnny Carson's Final Address on his
>   last appearance on the *Tonight Show*

By the early nineties Carson was beginning to feel the heat from his young late-night competition. Advertisers wanted chat shows aimed at the younger end of the market, the under thirties, and hosts like David Letterman and Arsenio Hall fitted the bill perfectly. Carson was well aware of the fate that had befallen his heroes, like Jack Benny who had been clinically removed from television. A comedian who had appeared on the show told his friends, 'When you go on that show, you can smell the polyester.'

When Carson's 39-year-old-photographer-son Rick died in a freak car accident in 1991 some of his personal life was revealed to the cameras as he chokingly paid tribute to him, adding, 'These have not been the happiest several weeks.' *People* magazine noted, 'For perhaps the first time ever, Carson's pain was visible. In a mere month, the sixty-five-year-old host seemed to have aged a decade. Then in the show's final moments, Carson broke with years of deliberate silence about his family to present a touching tribute to his son.' He described his second son as an 'exuberant young man, fun to be around . . . He tried too darn hard to please'. The show ended with a family photo of his son (the papers had been using a driver's licence shot) and then Carson showed some of his son's landscape photographs. *People* magazine summed up, 'For Carson, Rick's eulogy also meant revealing to approximately twelve million viewers a piece of his inner self.'

On 23 May 1991 NBC was parading its full roster of stars to advertising agencies and NBC affiliate stations at New York's Carnegie Hall. Their top news anchorman Tom Brokaw interviewed President George Bush by satellite whilst Bill Cosby, Jay Leno and Ted Danson provided the laughs. The audience however were completely unaware that the show was to be closed by Johnny Carson – and so were most of the NBC staff. His presence was only known to a few executives in the senior hierachy. The man who was the single most powerful generator of money for NBC, or indeed any other television network, was about to drop a major bombshell on the audience.

In between his succession of gags he mentioned this would be his last year as host of the *Tonight Show*. Most members of the audience doubted they had heard him correctly, top executives exchanged puzzled looks but as the monologue and the laughs flowed on most assumed it had been merely a verbal aberration. But then Carson got down to basics and blithely announced, 'And so we're going to go into next May and my last show is going to be May 22nd, 1992.' This was news even to the president of NBC, Bob Wright, who was due to dine with Carson that night. The only person who was party to Carson's decision was his wife Alex. After thanking the assembled throng for their support over the years and advising NBC to keep the show going with new talent he was gone, leaving flustered staffers to cope with one of the biggest stories in the history of television. In true 'Master of Showbusiness' style he had pulled the rug away at one of the top TV junkets of the year.

Carson knew that TV audiences now counted not in terms of quantity but spending power and his ageing audience held little appeal for youthful advertising. Not far from Carnegie Hall David Letterman was in the middle of taping *Late Night* when news reached him of Carson's announcement during a commercial break. The idea of him attaining his Holy Grail – host of the *Tonight Show* – was only just sinking in when Carson dramatically appeared on stage wielding a giant cheque of the type used by sidekick Ed McMahon on commercials for Publishers Clearing House. 'Ed couldn't be here, so he asked me to deliver this,' said Carson. 'Oddly enough, it seems you are the million dollar winner.'

The king was dead, long live the king. Carson it seemed had bestowed his crown on the new king of late night, David Letterman. Unbeknown to both men, however, just seven days before Jay Leno had signed a $6 million dollar contract with NBC guaranteeing him the *Tonight Show* job when Carson stepped down. The contract was kept a secret, with NBC stating that nothing would be planned until Carson completed his final year.

Carson had been at the cutting edge of television for over 30 years and he was determined to leave at the top. The final three months were a majestic descent from the throne by the king who saw the world of showbusiness come and pay homage to him. Most tellingly, his replacement, Jay Leno was not one of them. He simply wasn't invited. The final week's guests, Robin Williams, Elizabeth Taylor, Steve Martin, Mel Brooks and Bette Midler provided a stellar end to his career. He closed the book on 22 May 1992 in front of a studio audience of family friends of both cast and crew. His debut run in 1962 attracted an average nightly audience of 7.5 million. By the year of his departure this had risen to 32 million. At his leaving his annual gross income was estimated at $40 million with his *Tonight Show* contract making up half that figure. His final contract allowed for just 111 shows a year with fifteen weeks paid holiday. The revenue generated by the show accounted for almost 15% of NBC's total income.

To TV insiders Carson appeared to be the polar opposite of his *Tonight Show* persona. Moody and bad tempered before showtime he turned on the charm the instant the cameras were switched on. On air Carson was the epitome of showbusiness but his tumultuous private life and divorces were constantly subject to press intrusion. His common touch enabled him to make jokes at his own expense on the show to match what America was reading about him in the trashy tabloids. He married his first wife Jody in 1949 but still enjoyed life on the party circuit.

When his career began to take off in New York in the late 1950s he became a workaholic and his marriage to Jody began to founder. He divorced her and in 1963 married Joanne Copeland, moving into the plush United Nations Plaza in New York. The honeymoon didn't last long. In June 1972 he divorced Joanne and took up with Joanna Holland, almost twenty years his junior, whom he married shortly after. This marriage lasted almost ten years but ended once more in divorce in 1985. He married for the fourth time in 1987 to a woman close to half his age, Alexis Mass.

In April 1992 guest Jerry Seinfeld was amazed when Carson told him during an advert break that he was finding leaving difficult. 'I can't imagine someone telling me that I'm not going to have a relationship with a live audience anymore. I mean, it really becomes like a marriage in your life. You have this love affair with the audience, and you work for them, and they support you.' On a separate occasion he confessed, 'If I had given as much to marriage as I gave to the *Tonight Show*, I'd probably have a hell of a marriage.'

EAMONN ANDREWS

In the 1980s Eamonn Andrews stood as the lone survivor of television from the pioneering days of the 1950s when men wore evening dress, women dressed with decorum and all programmes looked like they were being presented in front of a giant stage curtain. Andrews' genial, warm-hearted Irish persona had ridden through the swinging sixties and shocking seventies to remain a constant with viewers, reassuring them that all was well despite the reality of life outside their front door (a role later filled by Terry Wogan). His early death from heart failure in November 1987 was to many like losing an old friend, someone who had been there since they first saw television.

Eamonn entered broadcasting whilst still employed by the Hibernian Insurance Company in Dublin. He wrote to Radio Eireann at the age of sixteen to offer his services as a boxing commentator – a sport which he not only knew about but also practised. He was taken on and described later his feelings: 'I wasn't nervous at all: after all, I was practically invisible in that glass-fronted box on the balcony. Radio I knew was perfect for me.' On the night he won the Irish Junior Middleweight title he commentated on all the preliminary rounds not featuring him and then calmly stepped into the ring to win the title. He later graduated to coverage of all sports, began to pen short stories, produced documentaries and fronted a children's keep-fit show.

His first experience of personality interviewing came with

Microphone Parade, a show where he tracked down celebrities staying in Dublin. His big break came as host of the quiz show *Double or Drop*. Irish cinemas could avoid Entertainment Tax if they provided live entertainment as part of their cinema bill. *Double or Drop* (later adopted by Andrews when he hosted *Crackerjack*) was a simple quiz: contestants doubled their winnings in stages up to £1 or risked losing all with a wrong answer. Andrews toured cinemas across Ireland with the show and soon became a nationally known celebrity. 'The show gave me invaluable experience in keeping my wits about me, to be ready for unexpected answers and quips, or help the tongue-tied or give someone a clue.' A young Peter O'Toole was an early contestant.

Andrews moved to Britain shortly after the war to try his luck with the BBC, but also in an attempt to break into the movies as an actor. He failed in both respects and returned to Ireland to continue with *Double or Drop*. In 1949 band leader Joe Loss toured Ireland and caught Andrews and the show. Loss offered him a slot on a UK tour with the quiz and soon after a BBC audition he found himself employed as quizmaster on the long-running show *Ignorance is Bliss*. Radio fame came quickly as he hosted *Housewives Choice*, *A Book at Bedtime* and became a mainstay of *Sports Report*. *The Pied Piper*, a music show interspersed with celebrity interviews provided opportunities to meet Noël Coward, Bob Hope, George Formby, Lena Horne and Norman Wisdom.

His ascendancy as television's number one front man was confirmed by his hosting of the panel game *What's My Line*, the most watched show on television in pre-ITV days, registering in 1952 a viewership of 90% of all television watchers. The simple idea of a celebrity panel identifying the occupation of a contestant was major news each week; front-page stories were devoted to Barbara Kelly losing her earring or Bob Monkhouse wearing an eye-patch because of a burst blood vessel. *This Is Your Life*, the programme he became synonymous with, began in 1955.

In 1960 he assumed the chairmanship of the independent body preparing to take over Irish broadcasting. His aim at this time was to launch a chat show, Johnny Carson-style: 'For years I had been pestering Ronnie Waldman [BBC light entertainment chief] to let me do a late-night talk show along the lines of those in the States which had cleared the way for King Johnny Carson to become a confident, smiling, talking millionaire. At one stage Ronnie told me – in all seriousness – that it would not be politic to have such a late-night show in Britain as it might keep the workforce up so late at night they would not clock in the next morning!'

Matters came to a head in the summer of 1964 when the BBC dropped *This Is Your Life* from the schedule, a decision that riled Andrews who believed the show had plenty of mileage left in it. ABC Television didn't hesitate to swoop when his rancour became known. The man who had been an integral part of the BBC in both radio and television throughout the 1950s and early 1960s joined ITV, becoming the very first TV personality to quit the BBC for its rivals. He was to host their new show *World of Sport* and more importantly was given his own chat show to be broadcast on Sunday nights in a deal worth £120,000 for three years. Such was his association with the BBC, as he busied himself in work for *World of Sport* in the back of a taxi one day, he discovered the driver had taken him to BBC Television Centre in Shepherd's Bush.

He soon discovered in commercial television an attitude quite different to that he was used to: 'The world of independent television was tougher and tighter – a world with no cosy, lazy corridors. It was a harder, headier, more dangerous atmosphere than at the BBC. One felt people could be fired for doing a bad programme, whereas at Television Centre the most that would happen would be a belt of a memo, or a long period of contemplation in your office away from the studios.' The chat show was a first for British television and very much uncharted waters. The idea was instigated by ABC Programme

Controller Brian Tesler after seeing the *Jack Paar Show* in the US. To be broadcast live, it aped the US formula with each guest appearing individually and then joining in as a free-for-all after their main interview was complete. Producer Malcolm Morris knew the enormity of his task: 'Eamonn saw the show as an exciting challenge, and like everything else he approached he was painstaking. I suppose both of us were nervous as we were exploring completely new territory'.

Andrews decided to stay in his dressing room before each show and not meet his guests until transmission time to allow a vital spark to develop on air. In an interview with Barry Norman, then a journalist for the *Daily Express* he was well aware that ATV were expecting him to shift from his relaxed BBC persona to an opinionated host, so the show became more contentious rather than a cosy parlour game. 'I have two choices – either to assert myself or to withdraw if the conversation is good without me. I'm still not sure if it's a good idea to protect myself too much. And certainly I shan't make an acrobatic, extrovert effort to pound the table and cry, 'Hear ye . . .' The devoutly Catholic Andrews was made a member of the Papal Knighthood of St Gregory in that year.

Britain's very first chat show debuted on Sunday, 1 October 1964 at 11.05 p.m. The guests on that historic night were Sugar Ray Robinson, William Rushton, Terry-Thomas (later to be a guest on the very first *Parkinson*), Honor Blackman, the Nocturnes and Sandie Shaw. The series began with damning reviews which followed throughout its run. Maurice Wiggins in the *Sunday Times*: 'It was a throwback to the emptiest sort of jolly-jolly pre-Coronation TV – when it was believed to be enough just to have people appear. Mr Andrews trying desperately to get a topic going – "Does the studio audience like men with moustaches?" – that was a sad sight. The paid guests kept giggling loyally, but at what, I never discovered. In sum, we learned that Terry-Thomas owns several waistcoats, Honor Blackman is afraid of spiders, William Rushton can imitate a squeaking door. There was a teenage beat group and a teenage pop singer who all made very unpleasant noises, which everyone present, being either with-it or scared of not being with-it, politely applauded. I've been at livelier wakes.'

Andrews was sanguine about the whole thing: 'There are some things in showbusiness nobody can teach you. No one can teach you, for instance, to be a good disc-jockey, a really good sports commentator or a talk-show host. I guess I made all the mistakes on the *Eamonn Andrews Show*: telling jokes I didn't believe in; reading scripts when I should have been free-wheeling; keeping to a question line when I should have taken off into the unknown; listening to my next question instead of the current answer; forgetting that nine out of ten guests are more nervous than their host. Gradually it became more fun, more relaxed. The super Teddington studios, the eager audience, the swish, rich sound of Bob Sharples and his orchestra, the whole team concentrating on that one world of the show itself, as if nothing else mattered inside.'

The show continually flirted with controversy. On one show Jimmy Edwards explained that his voluptous handle-bar moustache was a reliable indicator of his attractiveness to women. Throughout Andrews sat bemused and seemingly embarrassed by the whole affair. The ITA took a strong line after this particular show, issuing the statement, 'We and ABC both feel that last Sunday's conversation in the programme, even though transmitted very late and of course live was more outspoken than we would have wished. We have consulted ABC, the company which produced the show, with a view to avoiding such conversational excesses in future programmes. Before future programmes guests will be asked not to go too far. The producer will not ban any subjects but will authorise guests not to let the conversation get out of hand.'

Esteemed TV critic Peter Black in the *Daily Mail* was appalled: 'I return to Sunday's *Eamonn Andrews Show* impelled by the duty to protest against the level and amount of smut it tolerates. I can't quote the remark made by Jimmy Edwards to an innocent remark by Barbara Kelly. I can only say that it was a double-entendre well inside most person's capacity to spot. I could hardly believe my ears. Every regular watcher of this show knows that smut, sometimes funny, but nearly always juvenile, is offered far too often as a substitute for wit and conversation. It is always a threat in any live talk show that goes out late at night and has no special objective other than that summarised in *TV Times*: "When famous, frank and funny people meet, anything can happen". But this really beat anything I ever heard on it before. I half expected Barbara Kelly to walk out. It called on this kind of response.'

Diana Dors was nonplussed by events: 'I was not offended by Jimmy Edwards' moustache joke. I thought it amusing. Nobody is asking anybody to look at the show. If it offends certain people the answer is to switch off. To succeed, a show like this, which is based on conversation, must create all kinds of excitement. I think the ITA's decision is a shame.' The host also appeared baffled. 'The critics claimed Jimmy Edwards made me blush with some of his heavy-lidded double-entendres and, without being immediately aware of it, I was being built up as a very shockable character who shouldn't really be asked to mix with such horrible guests. The inevitable side-effect, of course, was that many a guest shouted the equivalent of "knickers", possibly in the hope that I would rush off in horror, but more in the stone-cold certainty that it would make the headlines. I was often told that I should exercise more discipline, more authority.'

The show featured a parade of 1960s hipsters who flaunted their credentials in the face of their blushing host. Photographer David Bailey used the dreaded 'C-word' ('crap' that is); actor Laurence Harvey lit up the switchboard when he calmly strolled off the set and, in front of Bob Sharples and his 'rich sounding' orchestra, launched into what a contemporary newspaper report called 'the most tasteless joke about a camel and the foreign legion'. Swinging London regarded the show with derision. Eamonn's wife, Grainne, and his mother overheard Barry Norman (then a journalist) interviewing songwriter Lionel Bart in a trendy London eaterie. He wanted to know why Lionel had refused all offers to appear on the *Eamonn Andrews Show*. Bart let fly with his opinion on the show: 'What does Andrews know about life? What does he know about anything, except his wife and kids, he don't go anywhere.'

Brian Tesler felt that criticism of Eamonn was completely unfounded and that guests were playing up to his gentle nature to cause him embarrassment. Malcom Morris thought the opposite, claiming the gaucheness was an act in order to play straight-man to lively guests. George Melly, then the TV critic of the *Observer*, agreed that Eamonn's demeanour was contrived: 'I've gradually reached the conclusion that, for all his air of a Newfoundland puppy desperately wagging its tail in the forlorn hope that the pool on the parquet floor will escape notice, he is less at his guest's mercy than he pretends to be.'

The ITA had had more than enough of the late-night raving on commercial television and the show began to be recorded before transmission. When Marianne Faithfull and Lord Boothby appeared, to discuss the use of marijuana, the section where Boothby claimed his trial usage of the drug had proved unenlightening was eliminated from the final programme. ABC began to lose its nerve, lest any action on the shows should jeopardize their position in the reallocation of television licences due for consideration by the ITA. Maurice Wiggins claimed the show lost impetus with this emasculation: 'The whips are out and without its fortuitous touches of titillation the show is desperately dull. I wonder what Mr Andrews, pre-eminently the family favourite in his BBC days, really thinks of his new show's notoriety. It's like seeing Barbirolli compering *Top of the Pops*.'

Despite the critical mauling, the standard of guests booked on each show was exceptional. One programme in May 1966 featured Noël Coward, Lucille Ball, Dudley Moore and Muhammad Ali. Andrews had upset Ali in an interview by continually referring to him as Cassius. Not the last time a British chat-show host would upset the boxer. Ali kept him firmly in his sights and the BBC were forced many times to re-edit Ali broadcasts when he continually referred to their former doyen of sport. Andrews could, however, show a certain skill in handling tricky subjects and guests. One show tackled capital punishment with the eclectic selection of Duncan Sandys, Dora Bryan, Peter Cook and Dudley Moore.

However, Peter Black at the *Daily Mail* was not impressed: 'No matter who goes on it, he becomes a silly and supernatural version of himself. If we had Shakespeare on, Eamonn would get him talking about the time he caught Ben Jonson trying to put his left foot into his right boot, and would change the subject if William began to explain what he was getting at in the sonnets.' Maurice Wiggins had some tips for Eamonn in his *Sunday Times'* column in October 1966: 'Sunday, the longest day, now once more closes with the *Eamonn Andrews Show*, that innocent celebration of the unformulated dogma, the subconscious certitude, which lies at the heart of showbusiness mystique – namely that "showbusiness personalities", like gods, are not required to say anything interesting to arouse proper feelings of awe and blessedness in lesser mortals, they need only appear and look benign. To correct this impression, Mr Andrews should watch *The Frost Programme*.' When he clocked show number 100 in February 1967 Andrews struck out against his critics on air by listing all the Fleet Street hacks who had slated the show. Peter Black was not deterred in his column that week: 'One technical quality I can admire is the consistently simple level of the questioning. If Shakespeare, Michelangelo, Shaw and Queen Elizabeth could by some agency appear on it, they'd find themselves discussing not their life's work but whether they slept with their beards outside or inside the bedclothes.'

In September 1968 the show moved from Sunday to Thursday but Andrews was not perturbed in those distant pre-VCR days: 'I think it may make a big difference in the viewing figures. On Sunday night, there were too many people who had to got to bed early because they were afraid of that awful Monday morning feeling. Thursday may be different. They are looking forward to pay day and the weekend and they feel in a very relaxed mood. I hope to get a regular audience of at least ten million'.

Andrews was no stranger to prolonged critical abuse despite his immense popularity with viewers but the shift to a current affairs/magazine role with *Today* gave his career a new impetus away from the pressures of late-night showbiz entertainment. 'The *Eamonn Andrews Show* often frightened me. Many critics said it frightened the life out of them too. But the fact is it would have run for many more years had the ITA not changed the style of contracts so that ABC died. Thames Television was born, and I became a weekday man instead of a weekend one. I loved a cartoon at the time, showing two old gents chatting in front of a newspaper poster which read, "Britain can take it", with a caption underneath, "Eamonn Andrews Show to run three times a week".'

'I was over-produced at the time and given the wrong kind of research but I was worried about using all the research I got. Now I know that you don't use it all. You just have it or you don't have a question line in your head before you sit down. It's too rigid. I know my work suffered from that, but we got nearly anyone we wanted for the show. I saw it coming anyway, I did get five good years out of the show and learned a thing or two about chat-show techniques. They (the critics) decided I was a shockable person, which I'm not really. The guests probably thought that if they could shock me they might make the headlines next morning and I suppose some people used to watch the show to be shocked. My only concern was to send the viewer to bed happy. I agree that early on it was nerve-racking, but the more experienced I became the better I was able to handle the guests. Some savage things were written about me; that's one of the sad things about this kind of journalism: they decide on your image and go on repeating themselves.'

The show retired in 1969. Eamonn then brought the big red book to ITV. 'How *This Is Your Life* – or "The Life" as the team called it – survived in Britain to be the institution it was has always remained a mystery. Small boys would shout the title at me across the street. Waiters murmured it as they pushed menus under my nose. Total strangers took dares for rushing up to me in pubs, airports, theatres, with anything from a red telephone book to a red handbag, and stumble out the magic words.'

> *The Show That's Dying Of Shame*
> *Evening News* headline, March 1979

The *Eamonn Andrews Show* was revived by Thames in the early eighties and like its sixties precursor was ripped apart by the critics. Broadcast from the stage of the New London Theatre and transmitted live it lacked intimacy. The show was only screened by Thames and Tyne-Tees and made headlines after the first two shows were unmitigated flops. Lord Longford was dropped as a potential guest in case he wasn't light-hearted enough and producer Stella Richman quit after just two weeks. Too add fuel to the fire as the show staggered on to the air, the BBC announced they had abandoned plans to stage a nightly chat show. Margaret Forwood in the *Sun* saw Andrews as the cause: 'I imagine that all those who protested against the plan, be they members of the public or the BBC board of governors made their decision immediately after seeing the *Eamonn Andrews Show*. I just wish for the sake of those viewers in regions wise enough not to screen the series, that I could do full justice to the true awfulness of Eamonn's weekly excursions into the West End in search of people who make the news.'

Andrews put a brave face on the show's reception: 'There are obvious dangers in doing the show live, but I enjoy them and so do the viewers. Live television is exciting and you have to accept that sometimes things go wrong. My old chat show faced its problems and once had to fade out Lord Boothby when he began talking about marijuana. It should be easier now. There are few subjects you can't talk about on television these days, and there is no kudos now in swearing on TV'. He would also deny that he had been shocked on his programme in the 1960s and claim it had been his duty to the viewers to be affronted. 'There is a danger in kowtowing but it is equally dangerous to be rude. You have to strike a balance. I'm not there to give people a grilling but to have a conversation to bring out whatever is there and to reveal new sides of people.'

Andrews later admitted he had fallen out publicly with the producer of the new show and felt stifled by the script. 'An experienced but moody scriptwriter was imported to write, among other things, funny lines for me. I had never felt very easy about this. David Frost goes out in front of a teleprompter and delivers a clatter of gags with the panache that has helped make him the success he is. But I tended to want to stammer and apologize, and explain that I'm reading off a teleprompter. I wanted to disclaim the jokes I had no faith in; and admit I didn't deserve applause for the ones that weren't mine.'

The critics were unremitting. Peter McKay in the *Evening Standard*: 'It has long been a source of wonder to people in the business that Eamonn still puts himself through the agonising TV hoop. He is a wealthy businessman, he can never be more famous. Why does he torture himself under the hot lights – panicked and often confused by excitable, sometimes weeping, showbiz folk?' Nancy Banks-Smith in the *Guardian* drew parallels with the 1960s show: 'It was a series which can be spoken of in the same bated breath as Krakatoa, Custer or the *Towering Inferno*, being a byword for popular disaster. Not so much accident prone as prostrate, Eamonn Andrews by combining the Celtic and the mechanical to a rare degree, became known to his admirers as Seamus Android. Thames said, "Eamonn Andrews talks to top people who make the news". Kenny Everett, Millicent Martin, Donald Pleasence and David Frost. It brought tears to the eyes to see the beads of perspiration still stand on Andrews' bothered brow as they always used to do.'

However, Bill Grundy, former *Today* cohort, sprang to Eamonn's defence: 'Having worked with Eamonn Andrews for many years I know he is far from the Seamus Android figure distorted by his detractors. Here are his weaknesses all of which he would be the first to admit: he is no great ad-libber, he is no great politico, he is no great pundit. Here are his strengths, and he would be the last to admit them: he has patience, kindliness, charm and an infinite ability to do what producers want. He is large, lovely and daft. Daft, because he of all people must know that he is the one truly unsophisticate left in showbusiness. There is no Mike Parkinson hairspray about Eamonn.'

Grundy's words sum up a host whose like will never grace TV screens again. Public service television had existed in Britain for 44 years (discounting the seven years of closedown during World War II) at the time of Andrews' death in 1987 and remarkably he had remained at the forefront of television for 36 years of its existence.

DAVID FROST

Hello, good evening, and welcome.
The Oxford Dictionary of Modern Quotations

To a generation born after the sixties David Frost is probably instantly recognized as the urbane host of the lightweight celebrity game show *Through the Keyhole*; or the anchorman for breakfast television at the weekends when the froth of the week gives way to serious political interviews. Few would be aware that he was one of the instigators of a revolution in television in the early part of that decade which altered the whole medium, almost simultaneously with the impact of the Beatles in pop music. In common with the Fab Four, he made his impact in his early twenties, found enormous success in this country and then the US, culminating in prolific activity as the decade drew to a close, before setting off on a more individualistic approach to his work. Bernard Levin would sum up neatly the Frost phenomenon: '"David Frost has said no memorable thing. Rather had the memorable things been said to him." That, David would answer is the very nature of the job he is doing. He is doing it with skill, vitality, perseverance and perception. A mirror of the age rather than a sage. A disseminator of views rather than a propagandist, a digger for truth rather than a builder of theory, he gives millions the opportunity to see and to hear with their own eyes and ears what they have no other means of finding out.'

The son of a Methodist minister Frost made his TV debut for Anglia in 1959 at the age of twenty in a regional programme called *Town and Gown*. He had won a state scholarship to Cambridge, entering the hallowed portals in 1958 after a short spell as a teacher. He threw himself wholeheartedly into the undergraduate lifestyle (at the expense of his studies: 'I arrived in Cambridge at five in the afternoon and by six I was in the swing of things') and became a member of the breeding ground of the future of British comedy, the Footlights. Contemporaries included John Bird, Eleanor Bron and Peter Cook. With Cook he undertook the writing and performance of the post-Christmas 1959 edition of *Town and Gown*, presenting a satirical look at university life. 'That special edition of *Town and Gown* was the first time I had ever ventured inside a television studio and I loved the whole process immediately,' remembered the budding satirist. In 1960 he became a television interviewer (off-screen) for the programme *About Anglia* and also freelanced for BBC East Anglia in their news department.

At this time one of the big ITV companies, Associated-Rediffusion, decided to trawl Britain's universities to discover one male and one female graduate to undertake a career in television. With his basic grounding in visual journalism Frost was successful and left Cambridge in the summer of 1961 armed with a second-class honours degree and a £15 a week job on the current affairs programme *This Week*. There he learnt the basics of how to put a programme together, from research to devising questions. He absorbed himself completely in the studio environment, studying not just his assigned role but that of all other facets of production, from cameraman to director, learning every aspect of his future trade. His experience extended further to off-camera interviews with the 'man in the street', until he moved to the entertainment division to front a show for the first time.

Let's Twist to Win capitalized on the dance craze sweeping the country at the time and allowed the novice host to tour the dancehalls of Britain to search for talent and promise female twisters the chance to appear on television. The success of the programme spawned trips to France with *Let's Twist in Paris* followed by *Let's Twist on the Riviera* (which provided him with a future Frost trademark, the *bon mot*, when he closed the show with a quote from Russian leader Khrushchev: 'The twist arouses the passion, inflames the lusts and is an enemy of the state'). His first review noted, 'David Frost introduced the programme well in quick throw-away sentences'. His producer Elkan Allan observed, 'His grasp of situation was instantaneous. He absorbed the most complicated instructions at the first time of telling and did not need an auto-cue.' However, the late William Rushton claims he once uncovered a Frost file of airport quips which included the 'I'm afraid it's caviare again, Mr Frost' line. The Frost persona, he said, was built around each anecdote prepared well in advance and then delivered with an air of complete spontaneity. Within a few months he had established himself as a potential force in television on the basis of a lightweight, throw-away show. Fame was just around the corner and the BBC were about to come knocking.

> **Satire** – the use of ridicule, irony, sarcasm etc. to
> expose folly or vice to lampoon an individual.
> *Concise Oxford Dictionary*

In January 1962 the producers of the BBC's enormously successful early-evening magazine *Tonight*, Donald Baverstock and Alasdair Milne, appointed Ned Sherrin to create a late-night TV show which could capitalize on the then-current boom for satire (spearheaded by the launch of *Private Eye* magazine and Peter Cook's Establishment Club). Sherrin decided to visit cabaret clubs in London's West End in the search for new talent. An advert in the luvvies' newspaper the *Stage* caught his eye: 'Noel Gay Artists congratulate brilliant young comedian David Frost on his cabaret debut booked at the Blue Angel for a week, retained for two months!' Despite his increasing TV commitments Frost had never given up his love of performing his brand of comedy to a live audience. Sherrin witnessed his act on 8 January and minuted Baverstock, 'Ex-Footlights (Cambridge), looks promising. Have seen him conducting press conference as cabaret turn at night-club where he was limited by the stupidity of the customers'.

His performance was impressive enough to allow him to be pencilled in as a comedy provider for the show with Brian Redhead set to act as host. As the programme was being brought together and the satire boom becoming louder, Frost still had to hold his day job with Associated-Rediffusion before the BBC made a final commitment. During this period he wrote and appeared in the five-minute preview show auspiciously titled *London Weekend* which showcased events in the capital that week-end. Most importantly he experienced celebrity interviewing for the first time when he hosted the film magazine *Close Up* where he chatted with Jane Fonda, James Mason and Robert Preston.

On 15 July the BBC finally shot the pilot episode of their satire show, now named *That Was the Week That Was*. Alongside a cast that included Bernard Levin, Roy Kinnear, Kenneth Cope, William Rushton, Millicent Martin, David Kernan and Lance Percival the show clocked in at over two and a half hours. During rehearsals Sherrin noted Frost's 'energy and multiplicity. He seemed to have a unique ability to switch from wild comedy to straight narration. David was the first of a new sort of television performer coming straight from school or university into the studio and absorbing camera and cue cards and inlay and overlay and run-up and feedback as the basic bricks of his trade.' The pilot with Brian Redhead anchoring was rejected but soon became a cult item at the BBC amongst back-room staff for an interview conducted by Bernard Levin with a group of Conservative ladies.

FIRST LADY: Mr Macmillan has always satisfied me.

SECOND LADY: It seems to me, Mr Levin, that anyone is rational if they agree with you.

LEVIN: That's one definition of reality certainly.

FIRST LADY: Mr Macmillan has always satisfied us.

THIRD LADY: Mr Levin, how would you like your daughter to be walking along a dark street at night and nothing done about it?

Fortunately for Sherrin and the team the ladies went to the very top of the BBC establishment to complain about their treatment on the programme and Director-General Hugh Greene saw the pilot. He liked it so much he ordered another show to be made with Frost as host. Shot on 29 September the green light was given for a series, with Frost handing in his notice to Associated-Rediffusion who tried to woo him with his own satire show. He hosted the debut edition of *That Was the Week That Was* on 24 November 1962. A revolution in British television was about to happen.

> *David Frost was fine as emcee . . .*
>
> *Variety*

In 1962 politicians were not the figures of fun as portrayed by *Spitting Image* nowadays. A cartoon in a newspaper was probably the limit of ridicule an MP could suffer and like those in the entertainment business at the time they could be assured that their elevated position was protected from any intrusion by reporters. The establishment and the class system were still defining factors in British society and woe betide anyone who dared to cross them by publishing books like *Lady Chatterley's Lover* or adopt a cynical tone when interviewing Conservative ladies from the shires. *TW3*, every Saturday night, broke the mould with its collection of topical sketches which varied from a spoof *Which*-style report, 'The Consumer's Guide To Religions', to outright lampooning of politicians. Prime Minister Harold Macmillan was impersonated by William Rushton and newsreel tampered with to give viewers the impression that the real prime minister had no idea what he was talking about. Politicians were not the only targets. Pop music, advertising and investigative journalism were all added to the irreverent brew, from a set which showed the entire layout of the studio. Cameras and sound booms were clearly in view alongside all the technical paraphernalia.

The series was an immediate sensation and David was at the vortex of the hurricane of change sweeping through Britain in his front-man role. Cabinet papers released in 1993 showed the immediate effect of the programme. Complaints from MPs had been registered by Postmaster-General Reginald Bevin, who was poised to take action before Harold Macmillan stepped in and minuted, 'I hope you will not, repeat not, take any action about TW3 without consulting me. It is a good thing to be laughed over. It is better than to be ignored.' The show was actually mentioned in parliament after MP Gerald Kaufman wrote a piece on thirteen MPs who had not made a speech in the House of Commons for ten years or more. One of the thirteen, Sir Norman Hulbert, Tory member for Stockport, complained in the House claiming breach of privilege and almost brought proceedings to a halt with laughter from both sides at the irony of his complaint causing him to make a speech at last.

As critic Willi Frischauer noted, 'The phenomenon of the show was this very young man, this "nonpersonality" (as he was soon described), taking over by sheer force of nonpersonality. Though not in song, he carried on where Millie Martin left off. The new face launched on three million viewers presented itself as a toothy sneer behind a quiff of hair, and a staccato manner of speaking in a precise, classless voice, with just the right intonation (a bit nasal) for a show with the declared objective of breaking down class barriers.'

The *Daily Mail* named him as the first 'anti-personality on TV'. Donald Baverstock, executive producer showered praise on the prodigy: 'David was the most remarkable man to emerge since television began. What television is about is conversation, of this David became the past master.' The country appeared to be gripped by Frost-mania. With twelve million viewers at the show's peak he became a household name almost overnight. Spotty adolescents would ask for a 'DF' at the hairdressers whilst the man himself received a letter: 'My son is aged four. When he grows up I want him to be a satirist. How do I go about it?' The so-called anti- or non-personality (take your pick) at the tender age of 23 was a TV phenomenon.

He described the feeling in his autobiography: 'The decibel level of the response to that third programme (containing the doctored Harold Macmillan film) took us all by surprise. Looking back now, the volume of outrage may seem surprising, but the mythical disgusted of Tunbridge Wells had never before seen authority, the established church and the Tory party treated as subjects for humour or mockery. Least of all the BBC, at a time when the growing number of television news bulletins were able to ensure that even "wives and servants" understood all the jokes. The whole thing was disruptive in the extreme. Fortunately for us, the majority of viewers shared our belief that these were appropriate subjects for ridicule. Occasionally, perhaps, they too were shocked by some of the earlier programmes, but shocked more by the realisation that somebody was saying publicly what they had been thinking privately.'

He made his film debut in *The VIPs* (1963) as a reporter in a scene with Richard Burton, Elizabeth Taylor and Orson Welles. He befriended them all and they later became regular visitors to his chat shows. In later years Welles told him that he always knew that David Frost would make the big time because as a complete novice he had asked director Anthony Asquith if he could redo a scene with his three stellar co-stars as he wasn't happy with his performance. Welles claimed he or his co-stars would never have dared to make a request of this sort to a director. He would revive his film career twenty years later with a role in the Peter Ustinov–Poirot TV-movie *Thirteen at Dinner*, as a chat-show host.

As the first series came to a halt in April 1963 the BBC Board of Governors decided the show would be renewed in the autumn but a closer eye would be kept on content. The first series had been allowed an open-ended running time but to cap this the BBC decided to schedule the thriller series *The Third Man* as the last programme on Saturday nights to tighten control on *TW3*. This was effortlessly circumvented by Frost as he summarized the plot of *The Third Man* each week, saving viewers the bother of having to watch it. Director-General Hugh Greene then ordered *TW3* to be the last programme each Saturday.

The show reached its peak on 23 November 1963: its entire content was a eulogy to President Kennedy (the day after his assassination) which garnered praise worldwide. This programme was recorded on US line standard and transmitted by NBC on both the following two days. Frost was exposed for the first time to the US public. In the US Congress, Senator Hubert Humphrey delivered the accolade: '"Art", said the philosopher Santayana, "is the trick of arresting the immediate". This program did indeed arrest the immediate. In all its ugly hardness but also in its searing tragedy, and in its depth of meaning in history, hope and duty. We have apparently been studied deeply – far more than from Friday evening to Saturday night, the time it took to write and produce the program. It is humbling to know what our friends think and hope. I wish to thank the British Broadcasting Corporation and through them the individuals who wrote and produced the program. I ask unanimous consent to have the BBC copyright transcript placed in the Congressional record.'

Despite reaching such artistic and acclaimed heights the writing was on the wall for the show. A sketch spoken by David in the persona of Victorian Prime Minister Benjamin Disraeli castigated the current PM Sir Alec Douglas-Home. The piece was one of the strongest attacks ever on a politician broadcast by the BBC and had to receive approval from the Director-General Hugh Greene before transmission. The show in which the sketch was broadcast on 19 October 1963 closed with a statement from David regarding the forthcoming election: 'And so, there is the choice for the electorate: on the one hand, Lord Home – on the other hand, Mr Harold Wilson. Dull Alec versus smart-alec.' With close to a thousand letters and phone calls of complaint regarding this one programme, the BBC took action and declared the last show would be broadcast on 28 December 1963, thus eliminating any influence the show might have had on the election called for 1964.

In the meantime the cast had travelled to the US to perform their Kennedy show in front of 18,000 at Madison Square Garden. NBC were so impressed by the format they took up an option to produce a US version of the show. Oscar-winning acting legend Henry Fonda anchored the show for the pilot and was no doubt surprised to see a review that declared him America's answer to David Frost. Frost, tellingly, was the only cast member offered a contract to appear in the US series, securing him a future when the British version ended.

Tory MP Sir Cyril Osborne was cock-a-hoop at the demise of *TW3*: 'I'm damn pleased. It wasn't English at all. There are things that Englismen and women hold as sacred, and they are against these clever dicks and their filth. I think I helped to kill the programme when I sent the powers that be hundreds of letters I had received from ordinary people who saw me on the programme. Everyone was on my side, you know. They are sick of sneers against everything that is nice and decent. If I helped to get it off television, I'm delighted.' Roger Wilmut, in his history of modern British comedy, *From Fringe to Flying Circus*, surmised the impact of *TW3*: 'For a programme which ran to a total of only thirty-seven editions TW3 made an amazing impact; indeed it still has a considerable reputation, although perhaps there is something of a nostalgic glow which has caused people to forget how amateurish it could be on occasions. When one watches the tele-recordings today, it is noticeable that there is nothing on modern television with anything like the "edge", even if the edge was a bit ragged at times.'

Frost's postcript for the series was: 'In social terms, *TW3* sprang to life at a time of rising dissatisfaction, in November 1962, untainted with the brush of the fifties. Increasingly, as a country, we no longer trusted the people whose business was leadership, who were born to rule, and who were older and knew better than us. Indeed, some of those with the most self-righteous outward moral tone were already exhibiting the greatest inner moral corruption. In London there were some other vehicles for this protest, such as *Private Eye* or The Establishment, but out in the provinces for a mass audience there was only *That Was the Week That Was*. Whether *TW3* triggered the mood more than the mood triggered *TW3* or vice versa is probably unanswerable. What is certain is the interaction between the two. *TW3* was probably one step or two or three ahead of what people were thinking and feeling, but not yet saying. It was never seventeen steps ahead. That would not have caught on: there would have been no expectant or receptive mood to tap. *TW3* was not some blinding light on the road to Damascus: it was a lens, focusing the light without absorbing it.'

On 1 January 1964 Frost flew into New York (the Beatles would arrive for the first time one month later) to begin a stint as London correspondent for the US *TW3*. He at once entered a heady atmosphere of chat shows, with Johnny Carson's *Tonight Show* being recorded in the same studio complex alongside the *Jack Paar Show*. Christopher Booker was with him: 'When he talked of Sullivan or Paar or Carson, he was more obviously star-struck than I had ever seen him.'

Do they get this show in Des Moines? – Audience member of US *TW3*

They see this show in Des Moines but they don't get it. – Steve Allen

> *David Frost, a song and dance man who can't sing or dance.*
>
> William Rushton

The seed certainly grew then to bring the idea to British screens. May 1964 saw a BBC one-off in the shape of *A Degree of Frost* which mixed comedy with the first foundations of a British chat show. A major coup was the first solo appearance on TV of Paul McCartney who answered Frost's probing questions on life as a Beatle. Shortly after, David Paradine Productions (named after his father) was formed and launched the interview format with an in-depth cross-examination of evangelist Billy Graham. With autumn approaching the BBC turned once more to the talents of Ned Sherrin to deliver a live late-night Saturday show.

Not So Much a Programme, More a Way of Life was planned as the *TW3* replacement, with Frost hosting a mix of comedy and most importantly a discussion format with the emphasis firmly toning down any hint of satire. The show had a long gestation period, with no less than six pilots being recorded, described by David as 'one – the soggy start; two – the getting the formula right; and then, just when most people were agreed that we had managed that, three – the Gadarene rush to self-destruction'. Debuting on 13 November 1964 (a Friday) the show put its emphasis on scripted comedy and unscripted talk and, in a ground-breaking move, was broadcast three times a week on Friday, Saturday and Sunday. Until its end in April 1965 63 programmes were produced and broadcast, all held together by Frost in his role as moderator for in-depth studio discussion on issues of the day.

Like *TW3*, however, the show ran into troubled waters with a controversial sketch based around the dialogue between a Roman Catholic priest (played by Roy Hudd) and a Roman Catholic mother (played by future Hyacinth Bucket, Patricia

Routledge). The priest solicits a donation for the church and inquires as to why the mother of 25 is not currently pregnant. She replies that her husband is not performing his duty every night because he cannot afford to get drunk. The priest then returns her donation to enable her husband to get back in the swing of things. Questions were asked in the House of Commons with Earl Longford referring to the show as 'that revolting programme'. The problems were compounded shortly after by a spoof musical based on the life of Edward VIII which was broadcast just four hours after the death of his sister, the Princess Royal. The series was not renewed and the knives were out for the host, who was subjected to a mock obituary in the *Daily Express* by Robert Pitman, headlined 'David Frost – A Short Life And A Sad Decline'. Most famously, Mrs Malcolm Muggeridge told her husband, 'David Frost has been sunk without trace', to which he replied, 'You mean he has risen without trace.'

The early part of 1965 saw Frost become a regular commuter between the US and Great Britain as he continued to guest on the US *TW3*. Recording on Tuesdays in New York, he was back at Television Centre the next day for rehearsals of *Not So Much a Programme*. At the age of 25 he declared himself a 'citizen of BOAC' (British Overseas Airways Corporation, later BA) and had become hooked on the US, 'and the generosity of a nation of immigrants to a recent arrival'. The rest of 1965 saw him taking a sabbatical to plan his future and, wisely, quietly escaping from the tag of satirist. He was determined to re-launch himself with a contemporary humour show but also to produce a chat formula for British screens: 'There was nothing in Britain comparable to Johnny Carson's *Tonight Show*. There was room for a talk show on British television fashioned to British needs.' The comedy show reached screens before the chat format when the BBC announced in September plans for a series called the *Frost Report*.

In the same month Frost would set about developing his

talent for self-promotion: he performed in cabaret for a London conference of representatives from US TV giant Westinghouse, advertising his potential with American audiences. The new year began with a headline-making breakfast given at the Connaught Hotel in Mayfair (7 January). A wide cross-section of society were in attendance, ranging from the Bishop of Woolwich to author Len Deighton. But the major impact was created by the presence of Prime Minister Harold Wilson (who according to legend only turned up because he thought Paul McCartney would be in attendance). As Christopher Booker noted in his book *The Neophiliacs* – A Study of the Revolution in English Life in the Fifties and Sixties: 'To appreciate Frost's achievements in gathering together this assembly of notables one has to reflect how, until but a year or so before, the Prime Minister of the day and a similar cross-section of public figures would have dismissed such an invitation as an impertinent stunt. What gave Frost the knowledge that his gamble would come off, was his intuitive sense of television's power to recreate the world on its own unreal terms – to reduce everything and everyone, politicians and pop singers, philosophers and journalists, bishops and entertainers, to the same level, as bit players in a universal dreamworld.' He was once more in the public eye with a brilliant publicity coup. This ploy was later revived in Bermuda in January 1972, when his US series was flagging. He flew 60 guests there for lunch, including John and Yoko, Bobby Fischer and Sargent Shriver.

The *Frost Report* launched on 10 March 1966, centering on a different subject each week. It brought together the cream of British comic writing, alongside fledgeling future members of Monty Python's Flying Circus. They included Keith Waterhouse, Willis Hall, David Nobbs, Peter Tinniswood, Frank Muir, Dennis Norden, Neil Shand, Dick Vosburgh, Barry Cryer, Barry Took, Marty Feldman, John Cleese, Graham Chapman, Eric Idle, Terry Jones and Michael Palin. The principal performers were Ronnie Barker, Ronnie Corbett and John Cleese, performing sketches

around what was known as a 'Continous Developing Monologue' performed by Frost.

> *I will not cross swords with peasants, but I will cross swords*
> *with England's bravest swordsman.*
>   Dr Emile Savundra

The chat show was finally launched as the *Frost Programme* with
David switching back to Associated-Rediffusion to launch the
ambitious three-nights-a-week (Wednesday–Friday) format. In
common with his previous work the pilot shows failed to deliver
any hint of what was aimed for but, when the show went live,
the hoped-for intensity was ignited. It was decided from the
beginning that the audience would be an integral part of the
production. As Frost explained, 'The use of a studio audience
not simply as a responsive backdrop, as it had been in "The Frost
Report", but as a key ingredient in the actual programme mix – to
be brought into the proceedings according to need. It's a familiar
enough idea now, but in the summer of 1966 it was thought
revolutionary. What we most wanted was the interplay between
the guests out front and a participating audience. We had always
intended that the new series would be live. The audience would
give it added electricity and unpredictability and authentically
too the interviewees would be speaking at a special moment
in time, in front of witnesses. There were certain remarks that
a politician could get away with in a one-on-one context, that
would be impossible in the face of a two-hundred-voice groan.
Two hundred was indeed the minimum figure we nominated
for an audience "quorum" – large enough for no one to be
too self-conscious, small enough to give anyone a chance to be
heard; the right size for a laugh not to sound like a giggle, nor
a gasp like a hiccup.'
   The controller of Associated-Rediffusion, Cyril Bennett, bet
him that the studio audience would take no part in the programme by the time the series aired. He was proved wrong from

the beginning. On 2 September 1966 viewers tuned in to the new format with the chance to enjoy loquacious actor Robert Morley in conversation. In previous private discussions Frost had discovered that the epitome of the English gentleman had an avid dislike of schoolmasters and was all in favour of closing Britain's schools to allow children to become self-taught. This idea in itself would have been enough to provoke a lively discussion between host and guest, but with a selection of teachers across the social class in the audience the level of 'chat' reached new heights. Frost noted, 'The presence of the audience – fluid and varied – had broken the hermetic seal between the studio and the public. I could sense that this sort of participating audience would demand more of me and my guests than was the custom. The arena was suddenly bigger and we were a little more naked in it, but the risks were well worth taking. We decided to dive in at the deep end and test our ideas from the very first programme. The result was the beginning of eighteen of the most experimental, and invigorating weeks I can remember.'

Every week the programme threw up a heady mix of guests and subject matter. US author Gore Vidal faced up to Tory MP and *TW3* fan Sir Cyril Osborne, a staunch supporter of corporal punishment. Mick Jagger discussed morality with the Bishops of Woolwich and Neasden. The studio played host to the gathering of Sir Winston Churchill's family, the largest number of relatives of the great man assembled in one place. Henry Barnes, the head of the New York Traffic Commission, toured London in a taxi and with the help of the audience attempted to solve the capital's motoring nightmare. Cannon Hugh Montefiore and philologist John Allegro debated the validity of the Dead Sea Scrolls. The Archbishop of Canterbury, Michael Ramsey, gave guidance on 'What I must believe to be a Christian'.

Two shows however proved to be watersheds for the chat-show medium in Great Britain. The first featured an interview with British mercenary Major Mike Hoare, whose chilling and matter-of-fact description of murder and carnage in Africa held both Frost and audience spellbound. The interview spread over the full length of the show with all other guests abandoned. As Willi Frischauer noted, 'It proved to David that viewers were prepared to listen to an interview lasting three-quarters of an hour, a discovery as important in television terms as Onassis's decision to build his giant supertankers was in the oil business. Few other interviewers had the strength and the authority to follow David's example.'

The second show emerged as a 'TV classic' in a roundabout way. Shortly after the tragic Aberfan disaster, in which 116 children and 28 adults died when a coal waste tip engulfed homes and a primary school, a group of psychics were brought to the studio, all of whom claimed precognition of the event. As Frost and the production team chatted to them before transmission time it became clear there was a degree of fakery evident, so the show was abandoned in favour of one guest, poet Sir John Betjeman. The risk was enormous: could David and his team hold together a one-hour primetime show based around poetry?

Betjeman asked the audience if they had any poetry of their own they could contribute. Frischauer recounts: 'And lo and behold, oblivious of the lights, the cameras, the other people, a little lady in the audience stood up and recited movingly, endearingly, some verses that she had penned under the impact of a deeply personal experience. The studio seemed to shrink into an intimate private room as others followed suit, revealing in verse some treasured mementoes they harboured in their minds. It was totally unexpected, it was life on television, exactly what David and his friends had hoped to create. Viewers heard and saw what nobody else had heard or seen before, the basic ingredient of good television'. Philip Purser in the *Sunday Telegraph* described it as 'the show in which The Frost Programme had finally, to borrow an atomic metaphor, gone critical'.

Christopher Booker, in his biography of Frost, suggested what lay behind his snowballing success: 'Everything to do with television really brought out the hidden shallows in Frost –

he had a gift for the telly; as soon as he came into a television studio something happened, he just was at home. It was the one place where he really could be fully himself: he had an intuitive gift for the power of television, right up to the point where he reached the Everest of his universe, the American chat show. I remember the first time he saw American chat shows. It was the first time I'd really seen Frost starry-eyed, he had at last seen the thing that he wanted to do, which was to be Carson, or Paar, sitting in the middle of that unreal little world that is the chat show. He set himself this goal, and all the way through the late sixties he just didn't put a foot wrong.'

The programme went from strength to strength. Rhodesian leader Ian Smith was interviewed (in sound only) to explain why his country had broken away from the Commonwealth. On one show the entire audience was made up of 200 children between the ages of six and ten. Another headline-maker was Foreign Secretary George Brown, who told Frost pre-show that right up to the last roundabout before the Wembley studios he was thinking about turning round and heading for home. In a frank interview he claimed to have no ambitions to become prime minister and that his close friend, former Labour party leader Hugh Gaitskell, did not have all the attributes necessary to be a successful prime minister. 'Harold Wilson knows how far you can go, when you ought to move, how you ought to do it. Hugh Gaitskell never had that touch and this is what makes a leader. The other man was a very distinguished man. I repeat much my closest friend but he would never have made a successful prime minister of the Labour party. It's a sad thing to say, but it is so. It's a question of knowing how to do it, and I haven't got this and I don't pretend to have. And you know, it's easier if one recognises it. Now, Hugh Gaitskell never recognized this, and I suspect if he'd been asked before he died, he would have said he was a very disappointed man. I, on the other hand, know I can't do it. So I'm not interested in that, whereas I know I can do other things. I can drive things through, issues through, and one makes one's own accommodation with life.'

The integral part of the show was when Brown turned to Frost and said, 'It's very odd to be discussing – it really is odd to be discussing things as frankly as this with you in front of an audience and cameras. It really is odd.' The newspapers raved about the interview: the *Evening Standard* said, 'Today everyone at Westminster hailed Mr Brown's performance as superb. Without doubt Mr Brown has now established himself as the warmest personality in the government.' The *Evening News*: 'Mr George Brown in a single dream of a performance on the telly has now shown himself to millions as the captivating old charmer many of us on the inside have long known he can be when he chooses.'

The show that has earned its place in the TV Hall of Fame came with the last of the series. Dr Emile Savundra had relinquished control of the Fire, Auto and Marine Insurance Co shortly before it crashed leaving thousands of motorists and their families with worthless insurance cover. Savundra, an arrogant, brazen, egotistical man, could not resist a confrontation with television's most famous interviewer. The studio audience that night was composed mainly of premium holders who had received no compensation from the company for the death and injury of relatives. Showing a complete lack of repentance, Savundra refused to answer questions from the audience, famously declaring, 'I will not cross swords with peasants but I will cross swords with England's bravest swordsman.' As the guest showed complete contempt for the audience Frost could be seen visibly quivering with rage, the show reaching its end. Savundra capped his appearance by saying glibly, 'This and other heartbreak stories have made me realize only too well that selling out was the wisest thing I ever did.' To which Frost replied, 'What do you mean?' 'By selling out I have no legal or moral responsibility.' 'You have no moral responsibility?' 'I have not.' At this point, as the final credits rolled in one of television's most famous moments, Frost was seen to be striding off the set barely containing his anger as a beaming but bemused Savundra stood in front of the audience.

The phrase 'trial by television' was immortalized by this particular programme and Savundra, after being given an eight-year jail sentence attempted to claim, unsuccessfully, at his appeal that the programme had influenced his trial. Frost summarized the incident succinctly: 'Trial by television was a clever emotive phrase. It had indeed become more of a slogan than an argument, and I do not believe that it accurately described either the Savundra programme or its motivation. Savundra was a singular, egregious experience. He offered himself, out of arrogance. The moth came to the flame, and was burned, who could argue that he deserved less!' Frost has never laid claim to instigating trial by television, only the occasional studio confrontation.

> *David Frost is a man for all ratings.*
> The *New Statesman*

The David Frost comedy career continued to flourish with the BBC. *Frost Over England* won the prestigous Golden Rose of Montreux award in May of 1967 and David Paridine Productions launched three hit comedy shows utilizing *Frost Report* regulars. Ronnie Corbett appeared in *No That's Me Over Here*, John Cleese in *At Last the 1948 Show* and Ronnie Barker in *The Ronnie Barker Playhouse*. Frost's star was in the ascendant. King of chat, comedy and TV entrepreneur, the *New Statesman* profiled him: 'His very lack of talent makes him king of the telly. In Frost the viewer sees himself – glorified but still recognisable.'

The autumn series of the *Frost Programme* followed on the success of the previous season with major interviews: John Lennon, George Harrison and the Maharishi Mahesh Yogi on transcendental meditation; MPs Brian Walden and Quintin Hogg debating the legalisation of marijuana; and the views of fascist Oswald Mosley. A major turning point in his career was registered on 18 March 1968 when he took over the *Merv Griffin Show* in the US after the host fell ill. He defied US chat-show strictures by delving deep with his guests and not letting the format run on its usual showbiz lines. Actress Susan Strasberg was drawn out on her study of psychiatry, whilst poet Allan Ginsberg was fiercely grilled on the subject of marijuana.

The summer of 1968 established him as a major TV name with eight interviews under the title *1968 – The Next President*. He travelled the length and breadth of the US interviewing Eugene McCarthy, Harold Stassen, Ronald Reagan, Bobby Kennedy, Richard Nixon, Nelson Rockefeller, George Wallace and Hubert Humphrey. The 90-minute format allowed each of the eight candidates nine minutes of interview time with Frost. After his assassination, Robert Kennedy's interview was shown on US TV complete with clapperboard inserts. Frost's foothold in the US was completed in July when he took over as guest host on the *Tonight Show*. At the same time Merv Griffin handed in a year's notice to the Westinghouse Group to quit his enormously popular syndicated chat show, join CBS and take on the *Tonight Show*. Frost's one-night stint on the show was not forgotten and his name figured high on the list of possible contenders.

In between making his name in the US, Frost was also part of the consortium bidding to take over the London ITV franchise for the weekend. *TW3* colleague Ned Sherrin noted, 'Before David no one in Britain understood that appearing on the television screen unblocks boardroom doors. David always intended to use television in every way possible right from the beginning.' They were successful in their bid and London Weekend Television went on the air on 2 August despite being blacked out for the first part of the evening. Frost was the cornerstone of the schedule, going out across the ITV network with *Frost on Friday*, *Frost on Saturday* and *Frost on Sunday*. Friday aimed to be current-affairs based, Saturday light-hearted comedy, and Sunday a mix of comedy and major showbiz names.

In his book *The Television Barons*, Jack Tinker dubbed the shows, Frost the Inquisitor, Frost the Laughing Ombudsman and Frost the Celebrity's Friend. The formula remained the same as the *Frost Programme* but it was clear that audiences were being chilled by too many degrees of Frost. The big names were still there: Peter Sellers, Sammy Davis Jr, Muhammad Ali, Noël Coward and the Beatles; and also the heavyweight stuff with the likes of Israeli Defence Minister Moshe Dayan and the former head of the Hitler Youth, Baldur Von Schirach. Despite this, in the first four weeks of operation the ITV weekend viewing figures dropped to their lowest since the service began in 1955 and the BBC were triumphant with a staggering market share of 61 per cent of the ratings. Lew Grade, who had lost the London franchise to Frost and co. but still controlled the Midlands during the week, called for emergency action and the show was fragmented throughout the ITV network, away from primetime and in some cases late evening. ATV replaced the Saturday show altogether with Dave Allan. Lew Grade was famously quoted at the time as saying, 'I got where I am by knowing what I hate, and I know I hate David Frost.' (a quote he later denied in a *Sunday Times* interview).

The shows ploughed on: Mick Jagger and Mary Whitehouse discussed morality; Ross and Norris McWhirter invigilated on attempts to enter *The Guinness Book of Records*; and Cardinal Heenan spoke on the Pope's encyclical on birth control, *Humanae Vitae*. But London Weekend was rapidly losing its way with the loss of its managing director and programme controller. Australian newspaper magnate Rupert Murdoch bought 36 per cent of the shares, but his attempt to take over the company failed when he was warned off by the IBA. Frost recruited John Freeman (former UK ambassador in the US and hard-hitting former interviewer of BBC's *Face to Face*) to run the company alongside former Rediffusion colleague Cyril Bennett as programme controller. The whole organization was steadied by their appointment and by April 1971 the IBA confirmed London Weekend was 'secure in its contract'.

I'm sorry Mr Frost but it's caviare again.
                    BOAC air hostess on one of his
                    weekly Atlantic crossings

In February 1969 the Westinghouse Group announced that their replacement for Merv Griffin would be Frost, who in a *Daily Telegraph* poll had come fourth in a search for the best man to be a dictator of Britain (Prince Philip, Enoch Powell and Harold Wilson led the rest of the field). Their offer was $2.5 million a year for five years to produce a Monday-to-Thursday show of 90 minutes duration each night. Frost fully intended to fulfil his London Weekend contract by supplying them with his three weekend shows (they initially balked at his transatlantic plans before relenting).

He undertook a long tour of the US to ensure that the 140 stations who took the *Merv Griffin Show* would take the *David Frost Show* and was branded in a teaser campaign as 'The Great Briton'. Against US TV convention he refused to have a sidekick and appeared as the main guest on the last *Merv Griffin Show* on 4 July 1969. A stockpile of interviews were created in Britain for the US debut, the foremost of which was with Prince Charles before his investiture as the Prince of Wales. In a TV first, the show was packaged and sold worldwide, a precursor to his Richard Nixon and Shah of Iran interviews. PR men and the press were astounded at the Frost style of booking guests; he rang them personally to cajole them on to his show.

US viewers were to embark on a stellar voyage of interviewees ranging across 750 shows when the series began on 7 July. They included John Lennon, Rex Harrison, Golda Meir, Lulu, Ronnie Barker, Ronnie Corbett, Frankie Howerd, Kenneth Williams, Charlton Heston, John Cassavetes, Peter Falk, Ben Gazzara, Jerry Lewis, Lee Remick, Tommy Steele, Spike Milligan and the Rolling Stones. The shows were an immediate success, with the Frost probing interview style a novelty in the US. A major story was the searching interview with black Congressman Adam

Clayton Powell, who made headlines with his claims of possessing secret information on the assassinations of President Kennedy and Martin Luther King. Much in the style of Jackie Kennedy, Mary Wilson gave viewers a guided tour of 10 Downing Street, a television first. There were memorable exchanges. He forthrightly asked Rose Kennedy, 'Tell me, when two sons have been gunned down by madmen, can you ever forgive?' 'No,' she replied, 'when that happens, however much you may try in your heart you can never truly forgive.' At that point a Budweiser ad cut in with the slogan 'Budweiser is the one beer to have, when you're having more than one.'

One critic trumpeted, 'The new David Frost dialogues are like rare beefsteak in a marshmallow sundae world.' As Frost outlined, 'There really was a talk-show formula in those days. The guests were almost invariably from show business, or authors with a new book, and they were generally allowed about eight or nine minutes before a commercial break gave them an opportunity to move down the sofa to make way for the next guest. There were rarely, if ever, any confrontations. Now we had a real confrontation (with Adam Clayton Powell) and it had lasted for thirty-nine minutes. During the interviews I had been doing round the country for the past few months, I had often mentioned that on occasion I planned to talk to somebody for more than eight or nine minutes – maybe even for twenty minutes. At such moments I could feel the Westinghouse contingent willing me to stop, or figuratively slashing their corporate wrists. What had they taken on with this guy? But now we had shown them one way that a longer interview could work.' A vital factor was Frost's control on the timing of the commercial break spots so as not to disrupt the conversational flow.

Jack Gould in the *New York Times* wrote, 'In the few weeks that he has been on the air he has introduced the element of intuitive reportorial curiosity and has proved to be an agreeable and sophisticated alternative to Johnny Carson, Merv Griffin and Joey Bishop. Mr Frost is too experienced a hand in show business not to realise that he must offer his quota of pure entertainers, and he does. But this necessary ingredient of TV programming really becomes secondary to the attractive and alert way in which he can draw out celebrities, including performers, so that in the course of ninety minutes the quotient of interesting substance is remarkably high.'

While launching his US career he hosted ITV's coverage of the Apollo 11 moon landing (trouncing the BBC) before heading back to the US for more shows. In one week in June 1969 he received an OBE, became a Doctor of Law in Boston and received the Faith and Freedom Award for communicating the relevance of Judaeo–Christian ethics to twentieth-century America. As the autumn season of *Frost* began on London Weekend his ocean hopping began in ernest.

In his 1972 biography Willi Frischauer highlighted a typical week in Frost's life in 1970. The US show went out five times a week to 100 stations, each programme running from 8 p.m. to 10 p.m. On Monday 14 September he shot two *Frost* shows back to back and then returned to his hotel to work on his book *The Americans*, a collection of his best US interviews. Sleep at 4 a.m. and then a 9 a.m. flight from New York to Los Angeles to begin rehearsals for a guest appearance on the *Dean Martin Show* in Burbank. With the show taped on Wednesday, it's back to New York and recording another *David Frost Show* on Thursday before catching the 10 p.m. flight to London. Arrives 10 a.m. London and drives straight to London Weekend to discuss the Saturday *Frost* show, an interview with Mary Wilson about her poems. 2 p.m. rehearsals begin for the show and at 9 p.m. Saturday he is there to greet Mary and Harold Wilson. At 10 p.m. the show is taped and he leaves for home at 1 a.m. A Sunday 8.55 a.m. flight to Frankfurt to interview Albert Speer in Heidelberg and then catching the 3.45 p.m. Frankfurt–New York flight via London. A 5 p.m.-to-6 p.m. stopover at Heathrow allows time for a business meeting before arriving in New York at 9.05 p.m., just 72 hours after leaving. On Monday afternoon he arrives at the Little Theatre to tape an interview with Vice-president Spiro Agnew and college leaders hostile to the Nixon administration. Three major interviews in three days give way to another show taped at 8.30 p.m. with journalist Bob Considine and author Truman Capote. Then a further interview with Commander Minuro Genda and Commander Mitsuo Fuchido who planned the Japanese attack on Pearl Harbor. Tuesday, acts as moderator at the Wagner International Symposium on public relations and the media before an audience of leading television magazine and newspaper journalists. At 6.30 p.m. time to tape another show with actors Art Carney and Pat O'Brien as the week ends later that evening at a reception for Senator Margaret Chase Smith at the Plaza hotel. His lifestyle at this time formed the basis of an episode for the Lucille Ball show *Here's Lucy*. An employee of the Unique Employment Agency she is assigned to 'mind' David on a transatlantic flight but contrives unwittingly to make the journey a complete nightmare for him.

He summarized his lifestyle at this time: 'Although I suppose it would have been difficult to do any more flying than I was doing – over the maximum for pilots, I was told – it was not like spending seven and a half hours during the rush hour on the Southend–Fenchurch Street line, or strap-hanging for the same amount of time on the tube. A lot of the time was spent in the first-class cabins of BOAC VC 10s in comfortable, albeit somewhat restricted, surroundings, and each time the destination – whether London or New York – brought with it a sense of excitement about challenges in store. Anticipation is arguably the best antidote to jet lag.' His London flat at the time bore witness to his intricate schedules, with a map of the world on one wall and clocks displaying the time in different cities.

His brand of chat show dominated both ITV and BBC when the BBC bought in the new-style US series which used the formula of a 90-minute show with just one guest. These included interviews with firstly Peter Ustinov and then Richard Burton, Elizabeth Taylor, Sammy Davis Jr, Spiro Agnew, Johnny Carson, Orson

Welles and Jack Benny, culled from a total of over 250 interviews in the series. The American formula was not popular with UK critics. Milton Shulman complained, 'This sort of stuff may be doing him the world of good in America but it is bound to diminish him powerfully here.' The American shows however still delivered an eclectic mix of guests. One show paired the ultra-conservative speaker on women's issues Clare Boothe with sex-bomb Raquel Welch. US critic Peter Heller described his interviewing style as like a 'bemused and slightly undernourished bird of prey transfixed by a being it finds too fascinating to attack'.

His autumn 1970 London Weekend season brought a stronger editorial style. He went head to head with newspaper magnate Rupert Murdoch after the *News of the World* began publication of the memoirs of Christine Keeler. Public opinion was against the series and the fee paid to Keeler after her former consort, Tory minister John Profumo, had retired from the public eye to engage in charitable work. Cardinal Heenan had recently withdrawn an article from the newspaper in protest. Murdoch underwent a tough grilling and told a reporter after the show that Frost had made an enemy that night and he was keen to re-instate his interest to buy London Weekend. A confrontation with self-styled yippie (a branch of hippiedom, so-called 'orphans of America') leader Jerry Rubin, made for more scintillating television. Rubin and his followers opened up on Frost during the show with water pistols. He left the stage to join the audience announcing, 'Your behaviour is a commercial for law and order.' The show carried on as he transferred to an adjacent studio. A debate on the ethics of the power-workers strike with members of the union brought forth comic dialogue equal to that of Peter Sellers in *I'm All Right Jack*. They claimed to be 'helpless prawns' and that 'when they offered us a 10 per cent increase we deducted.' 'What?' said Frost. 'We deducted that something was afoot'.

Another successful year in the US ended on December 19th

when he hosted a celebration of Christmas at the White House. The US show finally came to a halt in 1972 when Merv Griiffin returned to syndication.

David Frost's favourite places: *Home, a 747, Lord's, a Caribbean beach and almost any TV studio.*

Frost summarized his life on television up to this point in his autobiography: 'My first television programme Town And Gown at Anglia, had been transmitted in the last few days of 1959. That had been the sum total of my television CV prior to the sixties. All the rest had developed during the decade: learning to talk naturally to a camera, and indeed an audience, and not at it; separating the sketch that will never work from the sketch that, with some judicious editing, just might; learning that you don't go to an audience for what you can get more succinctly from an expert, but for what they are uniquely expert about – their own feelings, their own opinions, their own emotions; developing the different ways to transform an interview into a conversation; whether by relating the diffident, ruffling the complacent, or just by altering the body language; understanding that there is no such thing as a self-standing brilliant question in its own right – that a question can only be judged by the response it evokes. That's because the interviewer/conductor/host in a topical television programme of the type we have been discussing is first and foremost a catalyst rather than a principal. He orchestrates, he makes things happen. His job is to make the various relationships work: interviewer and guest, guest and audience, studio audience and home audience.'

Bernard Levin's epistle on the 1960s, *The Pendulum Years*, crowned him, 'Man Of The Sixties! How many coveted that title, sought it, wooed it, pursued it! One young man would perhaps be offered the title by many judges – not yet, but when the dust and the anxieties have sufficiently settled for us to see the decade's shape more clearly, perhaps David Frost grasped earlier than most the quality of the sixties. Always one jump further on than where he was expected, ever exploiting a new medium, a new technique, a new hairstyle, Frost divined by a remarkable instinct what the age demanded, and gave it. Young enough to remain for many years in the public eye, flexible enough to move on again and yet again, aggressive enough to battle on behalf of the future yet wise enough to keep on his side those who feared it, with all the most modern techniques for getting audiences and keeping them. David (as we may presume to call him lest we be constrained to call him Dave) at the close of the sixties could reflect, and probably did, that he had done well out of the decade, and that it had done none too badly out of him.'

The seventies beckoned with almost 30 hours of interviews with disgraced ex-President Richard Nixon for which he sold his LWT shares to bankroll the project. Nixon was paid $600,000 and 10 per cent of the profits for the four 90-minute programmes. A stipulation laid down before the interviews commenced was that a quarter of the chat must relate to Watergate. He admitted he had told some lies over Watergate but denied being involved in a conspiracy and confessed to letting the American people down. Clive James reported, 'Apart from the consideration that Frost is much nicer, Nixon and Frost are remarkably similar. They are both essentially role players at a level too deep for speech, they understand each other well.' The BBC alone paid £146,000 for the programmes which were bought by almost every country in the world.

In 1977 he hosted *A Prime Minister on Prime Ministers*, with Harold Wilson analyzing the careers of twelve of his illustrious predecessors. *Headliners with David Frost* appeared briefly on US television in 1978 with a mix of serious and superficial guests: the first show had the Bee Gees, John Travolta and former CIA chief Richard Helms. Part of the show, Headliners Forum, was more in the Frost style: a mixture of guests from different backgrounds would give their views (on film) to such topics as 'What is the secret of a happy marriage?' Major interviews ranged from writer Christy Brown to the deposed Shah of Iran in January 1980. The latter package was offered to NBC for £500,000 who turned it down after Frost had walked out on a previous interview with Henry Kissinger. ABC later bought the nine-hour marathon at a greatly reduced price. Asked at the time, he admitted his biggest interview targets after almost twenty years in the business were Greta Garbo and Howard Hughes. Regrettably the opportunities never arose.

TV-AM was launched on 1 February 1983 with David Frost, Michael Parkinson, Robert Kee, Angela Rippon and Anna Ford with its famous 'mission to explain'. His unique style was still to the fore as Stephen Pile noted: 'What his critics can never understand is that his very failings – a tendency to superficiality and an absence of clear values, gravitas or personality are precisely the things that make him a TV natural. Depth, scholarship, startling originality and commitment have never been prerequisites of this art-form. Furthermore, anyone who can still upset Margaret Thatcher and Arthur Scargill on breakfast TV in the same six months must be doing something right.' Other critics were less than happy with the show as Frost interviewed a woman who played tunes for customers on spirit bottles in her bar or conducted an interview with a 73-year-old woman who enjoyed swimming two lengths of a pool, backstroke each day alongside games of bingo and indoor bowls. James Murray in the *Daily Express* wondered what had become of the great man: 'Is this the man who took the nation by storm in the early sixties with his coruscating wit which ripped into politicians and left the Establishment trembling? Is this the man who reduced the discredited Richard Nixon to tears? Is this the first television crusader who virtually single-handed delivered the come-uppance of insurance fraudster Emile Savundra before a hypnotised nation?' When TV-AM was taken over, of the famous five he was the only survivor.

Yes, he thinks he's God almighty.
David Frost's wife, on being asked whether
her husband was religious

An excursion into the world of US tabloid television, hosting *Inside Edition*, was curtailed abruptly after executives felt his presentation and style was too dated. Critics in the US were appalled that someone of his television stature would be willing to enter the world of Geraldo and the tabloid television circus. As one remarked, 'It's something to do with the accent, we listen more carefully when people speak in a British accent.' Sy Yanoff, President of Boston station WNEV claimed, 'Frost is a throwback to the 1960s. You need someone contemporary to do a contemporary show.' The production company involved, King World, had ploughed $20 million into the series plus a promotional campaign costing $8 million dollars to cover the first two months. The show had its own 10,000 square foot studio in New York plus a team of fourteen news crews scouring the US for stories. The short-lived venture had projected 30 weeks work for Frost in the US and fourteen in Britain, where a purpose-built studio (identical to that in the US) was constructed in the TV-AM complex. His five-year contract came to a halt after just fifteen days.

Despite these setbacks he was the UK's highest-paid broadcaster in April 1992 with a reported salary of £9,000 for each of his TV-AM shows. In June, as TV-AM's franchise loss loomed, he moved to the BBC to host their Sunday morning *Breakfast Show* at a cut-rate £92,000 a year. A BBC insider revealed his name still had an instant effect when dealing with US contacts: 'The big names answer the phone to him. Nobody else can phone the people he can and get through – and they're pleased to talk to him.' His reputation was still unmatched, having interviewed the previous six US presidents (including Clinton) and the last five prime ministers. Labour leader John Smith once told him, 'You have a way of asking beguiling questions with potentially lethal consequences.' David replied he would be happy to have that on his tombstone. *Thatcher: The Path to Power – and Beyond* was a three-part analysis of the former Tory prime minister: 'It was absolutely fascinating to hear her talk about areas of life outside politics in real detail for the first time.' He also interviewed Bosnian Serb leader Radovan Karadzic and landed a scoop with *The Man Who Broke the Bank*, featuring rogue banker Nick Leeson.

In 1993 Carlton revived the *Frost Programme* format for the first time in twenty years with a live studio audience. After over 30 years in the interviewing business he still retains his place as Britain's pre-eminent inquisitor. George Bush gave him his first interview after leaving the Presidential office. When Bush and Frost both attended a Downing Street function in the late 1980s the US President strode up to Frost and announced, 'At last someone I recognise!' More recently, when told that Bush's office was on the phone, Frost asked a secretary, 'Tell them to have George call me at home!'

In an interview with the *Independent* shortly after his knighthood he answered criticisms that, because he mixed on a social basis with the great and the good, his chummy interview style was less than probing: 'I've learned a few new techniques over the years, as you hope one would. And most of those have been to do with drawing people out in a colloquial, conversational way. I think you have to be wary of the huff-and-puff question, which is there to make the interviewer look good. If you say: "Mr X, would you agree that your whole life has been a waste of time", you will get a reputation as a fearless interviewer, but it's actually an easy question for Mr X to answer. All he has to do is say: "Funnily enough I don't".' Frost remains unique amongst all other chat-show hosts, still top of his profession after almost forty years on television.

PHIL DONAHUE

He established the fact that women were interested in more than mascara. He set the standards.

Oprah Winfrey

The evidence is pretty overwhelming that as we move into the twenty-first century, Americans have more and more interest in Madonna and less and less interest in the Persian Gulf or Central America.

Phil Donahue

Although long usurped by Oprah Winfrey, Phil Donahue was the man who formulated and made successful the daytime talk show as we now know it. He brought debate on serious topics to daytime, providing a platform for debate on everything from politics to medicine. He brought with it the touch of the common man: 'We are dangerously close to being referred to as an intelligent talk show. If that happens, we're doomed. Call me outrageous. I'd rather be called sleazy than to be identified as intelligent.' With the proliferation of talk shows in the late 1980s providing even more sensational topics, Donahue was forced to adjust: 'We used to be the only kid on the block, swaggering around the mountaintop, and so we could feature programmes that interest me as a news junkie, things that our show was unique to present, public service and so on. We knew we could not keep the audience if we did not have variations on the theme of the male stripper.'

When Donahue, the paragon of serious TV, began to ape his rivals the change was deemed so dramatic PBS brought together a forum of TV critics to discuss the future of daytime talk shows. The extent to which his show had changed was highlighted in 1994 when he challenged state officials in North Carolina to televise the execution of murderer David Lawson. Lawson had exercised his right to invite witnesses to his execution and asked Donahue to tape his demise. He was refused permission and Donahue sued the state. He remarked, 'I would be pleased to have an execution on the Donahue show. What's wrong with it? Let's see future bad guys watch these people fry right here on television.'

> *We are asked to be a BBC media, and part of our job is to*
> *attract an MTV audience. I don't want to be a dead hero.*
> Phil Donahue

Phil Donahue's broadcast career began in the 1950s at station WNDU-TV in South Bend, Indiana, where he worked during his summer holidays from college. A succession of broadcasting jobs followed until he made his mark in Dayton, Ohio, where he worked for WHIO-TV as a news anchorman and host of an interview programme called *Conversation Piece*. His work as a journalist for the station attracted plaudits for items like his interview with teamster leader Jimmy Hoffa which was used on the CBS evening news. He became friends with a new programme director, George Resing, who was keen to launch a radio-style talk show for television with informative topics and guests but without the formalities of showbusiness. They planned a six-week schedule aimed specifically at female daytime viewers but trying to avoid the usual clichés of cookery and beauty tips. Donahue later defined his viewers, 'The average housewife is bright and inquisitive, but television treats her like some mental midget.'

The show debuted on 6 November 1967 and by the end of the week had become the talking point of Dayton. Subjects in that first week ranged from atheism and what men liked in women to interviews with an undertaker (Donahue appeared in a coffin) and a gynaecologist. But the real clincher came on the Friday when Donahue produced an anatomically correct male doll and invited viewers to air their opinions about it. The Dayton telephone system was overwhelmed and the Ohio Bell company demanded that the show should drop its advertised telephone number on air as emergency calls could not be made. By the end of that month Donahue had claimed almost half of the daytime viewers in Dayton. 'Issues are what saved us. We discovered women were out there in the daytime and dying for this kind of programme. There was tremendous sexism among the decision makers. They thought women cared only about covered dishes and needlepoint. I knew if we were going to survive with a visually dull format, with people sitting on folding chairs and two camera and no budget, we had to do issues that made people sad, mad, glad.'

Before Christmas of that year Donahue did something that in the history of the talk show was the equivalent of man learning to walk upright or inventing the wheel. Carried away by the debate on the programme he left his studio seat and mingled with the audience. Donahue found the atmosphere even more highly charged as he wandered amongst them, something the viewers at home could also see, and his immersion in the audience became an integral part of the show. An interview with an openly gay man was also a groundbreaker for the show. Within two years the show was being syndicated across America but noticeably not in New York where it was deemed too controversial. Subjects in that period included lesbian mothers, film of an abortion and a show from inside Ohio State Penitentiary. All very tame by today's standards but at that time very controversial.

Woman wins eight-year battle to care for disabled lesbian lover.

Donahue show topic

In 1974 the show moved to Chicago in order to expand and attract bigger showbusiness guests. Oprah Winfrey would replicate the move almost ten years later. Within five years the show was seen in 200 cities and was known as just *Donahue*. Newsweek told its readers that *Donahue* was the hottest talk show on TV, describing it as, 'part psychodrama, part street theatre, part group therapy and always "pure television".' In the mid-eighties when Oprah Winfrey challenged and took over the mantle of Chicago's top talk-show host, Donahue decided to move on and relocated to New York. In December of 1985 Donahue claimed a first when, with Russian journalist Vladimir Pozner, he organized a 'Citizens Summit' where audiences in Leningrad, Washington and Seattle exchanged views on world affairs and human rights issues. He immediately became a famous figure in the Soviet Union and was the first Western journalist to visit Chernobyl after the nuclear accident.

With the proliferation of talk shows on daytime TV, Donahue adapted from serious issues to exploitation. 1988 was a seminal year with Donahue dressing as a woman for a show on transvestites, appearing bald with a latex skull to investigate hair loss and, most notoriously, introducing a programme on the 'sport' of dwarf tossing. After his cross-dressing show he claimed, 'Sometimes you have to tapdance a little faster to draw a crowd. It worked: I got myself on the cover of *USA Today*.' In the 1960s *Newsweek* had jokingly claimed that Donahue's perfect guest would be an inter-racial lesbian couple who have had a child by artificial insemination. Ironically just such a couple appeared on the show.

When I think of sex, I think of Donahue.

Dr Ruth Westheimer

The show took on an even more bizarre angle in 1992 when Donahue pre-recorded introductions and inserts for programmes but did not appear at the live taping. Technicians raced around the audience holding out microphones Donahue-style for reaction. The result was total chaos and not appreciated by fans of the show. As the competition spiralled for more way-out topics, Donahue was asked by *TV Guide* where he would draw the line for his show: 'I don't know. We got here by being outrageous. We've televised an abortion, and the birth of a baby. I've wrestled women, belly-danced and was thrown out of a roller-derby ring. I've been body-wrapped, acupunctured. We are tabloid, I'm happy to wear the label. I believe there is a check and a balance. Our problem is not that we go too far, but that, generally speaking, the media don't go far enough. Those who go too far, too often, will fall of their own weight. People won't watch politicians or male strippers five days a week.'

His twenty-fifth anniversary celebration at the Ed Sullivan Theatre saw his disciples come to pay homage. They included Oprah Winfrey, Jerry Springer, Montel Williams, David Letterman, Geraldo Rivera, Maury Povich, Sally Jessy Raphael, Faith Daniels, Jenny Jones, Larry King, Mike Wallace, Connie Chung, Diane Sawyer and Dr Ruth Westheimer. Soon Donahue felt he had taken the entire talk-show format to the very limits and decided to retire, leaving his host of fellow players searching for even more outrageous themes. By 1995 he had tumbled in the ratings from third to ninth. He recently made the headlines once more when the Princess of Wales, on a tour of America in 1996 was intercepted on the dancefloor at a charity function by the man himself and against all royal protocol was taken in hand as a dance partner.

SIMON DEE

He truly is sincere to the point of naivety; the cynical world is not ready for him.

Allan Hall

I am strictly a no-talent man, I just don't have the intellectual capacity of David Frost.

Simon Dee

Simon Dee is unique amongst British chat-show hosts. Where all the others have thrived in their careers post-chat, Simon Dee's ascendancy lasted four short years at the end of the 1960s and he subsequently faded to obscurity. The British press love a showbiz failure and his fall from grace was nothing short of spectacular. The opening and closing credits of *Dee Time* epitomized the era as the host pulled up in his E-Type Jaguar at the top of a multi-storey car park to let in a willowy blonde girl passenger and then descend the spiral roadway in the style of the swingiest of swinging London films. This real-life person had all the appearances of someone acting out his life in some groovy scenario based around the fantasy life of a 'Top telly presenter'.

Dee summed up the period before TV fame: 'I'm not trained in anything really. I have no talent like playing a piano to fill the Albert Hall. I was just a bum actor, really, a layabout.' He had left Shrewsbury public school with just one O-level in Art. In the 1966 edition of *Who's Who in Pop Radio* his biography contradicts that statement claiming, 'Simon Dee is a man of many talents'. His achievements at the age that year of 28 listed designing ties and dressing gowns for the House of Dior and being a contender for the Olympic swimming team when he was a teenager. Born in Ottawa, Canada, as Carl Nicholas Henty-Dodd his career in broadcasting began during his service with the RAF in Baghdad when he worked for the British Forces Network and used all of his spare time to learn the art of radio presentation. After leaving the RAF he worked as a vacuum-cleaner salesman, bricklayer, toilet designer and owner of a Hampstead coffee bar.

> *A pleasant shining young man who reminds me of a fellow*
> *who used to come to our door selling brushes.*
>   Lord Ted Willis

He became the first star disc-jockey on pirate radio with Radio Caroline (adopting his son's christian name and the initial from his own surname) and consolidated his fame with TV appearances on *Ready Steady Go!* and *Thank Your Lucky Stars*. In May 1965 he left Caroline to become a freelancer and soon was the first 'pirate' to work for the BBC. He appeared on the Light Programme and also had shows on Radio Luxembourg. He was the number two DJ in the *NME* awards for 1966 and a regular *Top of the Pops* presenter, alongside his TV ads for Smith's crisps. He was a big fan of Tamla Motown but in true Simon Dee style, as one of Britain's top DJs, expressed a great love for the big band sounds of Tommy Dorsey and Count Basie. A contemporary profile hinted at his swinging image: 'Simon runs a 3.8 green Jaguar which is often seen parked outside Television Centre.' When *Dee Time* premiered from a former church in Manchester (the home also of *Top of the Pops*) on 14 April 1967, he was already a major name and very soon would be one of the hottest properties on television. He would look back on the following years somewhat ruefully: 'It's a very high point of reality talking live to your nation every week. It scares the pants off you. I was trained for that power, but people didn't appraise me. They saw me as a TV figure, and the jealousy was amazing – such a bitter emotion.'

Ironically *Dee Time* launched in the week that another transitory 1960s TV celebrity quit, the chirpy hostess Monica Rose who left Hughie Green's *Double Your Money*. The first show ended in tears for Dee. Bill Cotton and a team of TV top brass gave him short shrift for his wayward performance. 'Afterwards I just burst into tears and cried because I wanted it to be so good. Yes I cried, then I thought to myself here you are, thirty years old and crying because you can't do a TV show. But you see it was part of my plan in life. I didn't want it to be a goof.' *The Times* critic Michael Billington captured the essence of *Dee Time* superbly shortly after its launch: 'When he is not helplessly doubled up with mirth at his guest's witticisms, he is saying things to lady singers like "What's on the scene for you now?" In fact the whole show could easily be retitled Twenty Questions.' The *Guardian*'s TV critic Stanley Reynolds came to his defence in that he was so relaxed he showed he was a man in complete control: 'The difficult part about Dee's job is making it look easy and if people criticize him because he does not look as though he is doing any work, it is just that they do not understand the programme.'

> *The chat show, where a disc-jockey plays a few of his friends.*
>
> Frank Muir

Dee Time became a sensation, with its star proving he was a TV natural, appealing to viewers of all ages. The *Sunday Telegraph* christened him 'a bland nothingness', a description which could match 90 per cent of today's TV stars. The programme debated weightier topics despite its critical bashings for being too frivolous. On one programme Jeremy Thorpe discussed parliamentary

reform in a line-up that included Johnny Ray, Vera Lynn, Warren
Mitchell and Gina Lollobrigida.

> *How is it that this trendy, toothy, lion among the Christian
> names has, since announcing records on Radio Caroline back
> in 1964, become such an enormous success without, as far as
> I can judge, any visible talent?*
>
> Unity Hall in the Sun

In May 1967 with the show just four weeks old, Dee was receiving
over 500 fan letters a day. The show came into its own in September 1967 when it moved from the twice-weekly slot broadcast
from Manchester to London with the opportunity to attract
bigger showbiz names. The BBC backed its potential by dumping
the long-running *Juke Box Jury* and placing it in the primetime
Saturday-night slot after *Doctor Who*. At the show's peak in
1968 Dee's fan club members received a weekly 'Dee-notice',
called Dee-Votedly Yours, containing their hero's thoughts on
everything happening from politics to showbusiness. They were
kept aware of 'Dee-velopments' in his career in 'Dee-coded' form.
The Dee Code was issued to members and gave forthright advice
to all followers of the great man. Making love is not a sin
and drug-taking is weak-willed were just a few of the many
items of advice on offer. During this period he took it upon
himself to instigate a fund to pay off the National Debt and on
one Saturday-night show raised £2,500 that included his fee, a
minimal dent on his finances after receiving £9,000 for a TV ad.
On BBC2's *Late Night Line Up* Dee revealed that he only wanted
to be an actor and that *Dee Time* should be transmitted every day
of the week.

> If the BBC doesn't like Simon Dee's beliefs, then all
> they have to do is to sack Simon Dee. It's simple.
>
> Simon Dee

At the end of 1968 the series moved to Monday night. The

entertainment world was opening up for the host. He had written seventeen chapters of a part-autobiographical novel about a TV-show host who is being blackmailed and songwriter Les Reed (of Tom Jones and Englebert Humperdinck fame) had persuaded Dee to record one of his songs. Dee observed of himself, 'I'm a strictly non-creative person at the moment. This is my hang-up. I know I am creative. There is something inside of me waiting to come out. Whether it comes out in singing, writing, or acting, we shall just have to wait and see. I'm not going to stop until there is nothing left to do. If that sounds terribly egotistical I am very sorry.'

In October 1969 the BBC bizarrely renamed the show *Simon Dee Introduces His Guests* as they felt there may be confusion with their new heavyweight political programme with Robin Day, aptly called *Day Time*. Although his BBC career was now dramatically on the wane, *Daily Mirror* TV critic Clifford Davis was still full of praise: 'Simon Dee has done one hundred and fifty BBC shows, some good, some bad, some awful. But the programmes have been real television, live, off the cuff.' The axe fell in December when his three-year contract was terminated after the BBC refused to consider a move to a late-night slot to allow for more adult chat and entertainment. Dee had personally approached BBC Head of Variety Bill Cotton who refused to see him.

He had not become a millionaire as the anchorman of one of Britain's most watched shows, as would probably have been the case in later decades. His starting salary as a novice host had been £150 a show which had risen to £250 at his departure. The financial lure of commercial television beckoned but Dee graciously recognised the contributions of his backroom staff at the BBC that included writer Joe Steeples, researcher Patricia Houlihan and film expert Peter Noble. Dee's career was about to go into a rapid descent but his paisley shirts and loose interviewing style would become a lasting memory of Britain in the grip of flower power. With psychedelia in full bloom and reliant on a starburst of colour most of its seminal images from that period are fixed in black and white. The Beatles performing 'All You Need Is Love', the myriad groups on *Top of the Pops*, not least Procol Harum and Simon Dee's wardrobe. Britain may have led the world in style and music but, unlike America, which already had colour television and the beautiful images of San Francisco and Monterey there was still an air of austerity.

Dee was very much of his time. A naive innocent whose cool DJ talk somehow meshed with the celebrities of the time. As one critic noted, 'He became a mythic figure, still remembered as a byword for arrogant and premature celebrity. He is part of the cultural driftwood of the 60s, washed up occasionally on the rought tide of nostalgia.' Dee was laid-back regarding his talents: 'Spike Milligan, like Peter Sellers, is a genius, no arguments, genius. But people won't accept such a star for what he is and what he can do and be grateful. They always have to probe and find a reason. You see I'm so conscious of the fact that I can't do anything well. Oh yes I know I can control a programme: maybe that's a talent of sorts, but I haven't that kind of supreme talent.'

> *I am driving fast in a fog.*
>
> Simon Dee

London Weekend gave Dee what he wanted, more money, a late-night slot and the chance to broaden the chat element of the show and 26 were commissioned. He brought with him an audience regularly approaching ten million. 'The BBC dictated to me. They never let me do what I wanted. We were also dictated to by Tin Pan Alley. I would get someone talking on my show, and then, after a few minutes on would come the Tremeloes or some group. You could never get a conversation or a good scene going.' Quotes like this are the essence of the Simon Dee persona with the use of a phrase like 'Tin Pan Alley' (in the era of Woodstock, Led Zeppelin and progressive sounds) and describing trying to get 'a scene going'. He also claimed his BBC brief had been to let guests speak for just six minutes regardless of quality and that he had no leeway to bring a greater depth to the programme.

The ITV series became a disaster after the initial honeymoon period. By March 1970 the show had dropped from its initial viewer share of 19 per cent to 13, close to the all-time record low for ITV. A contemporary headline called it, 'The Most Sniped At Show On TV'. One critic despaired that Dee's style remained unchanged from his BBC days: 'The essence of Mr Dee's art is casualness. He has refined it to such a point that he reminds me, when standing, of a set of limp, long underwear and, when talking, of someone who is surprised at just recovering his power of speech.'

One of the first shows for ITV that caused the most furore was a line-up that included Black Power leader Malcolm X, sex-change personality April Ashley, John Lennon, Yoko Ono and the then current James Bond, George Lazenby. Lazenby dominated the first half of the show refusing to discuss Bond but making a rambling demand for a TV inquiry into the assassinations of John and Robert Kennedy. Dee appeared powerless to exert any control over his guest as the diatribe took over the whole first part of the programme. Sean Usher in the *Daily Sketch* questioned the fact that a show costing London Weekend over £200,000 in the next few years, and with a massive production team, could be sunk by a flamboyant guest that the show's host could not harness. Dee was unapologetic: 'Okay criticize. But 1.5 million people have now seen my shows, that's the total audience since I started, so I don't give a damn.' He admitted that Lazenby had fooled him and his researchers, making no mention of his forthright assassination views beforehand. 'So George made a fool of himself. Not me – he died the death baby, not me.' Dee bravely defended his choice of guests, including April Ashley who he claimed had been discriminated against. He declared that an interview with Des Wilson of Shelter had been derided by the critics. The direction he was travelling in seemed to hold no fears for the king of TV chat, 'It doesn't worry me baby. I'm running my show, not anybody else.' Usher made an ominous prediction in the footnote to his article: 'During the next five months of his launching run on ITV, Simon Dee will find out whether that forthright comment is a battle cry . . . or an epitaph.'

In June 1970 London Weekend cancelled *The Simon Dee Show* and paid its host a golden handshake of £10,000, in exchange for cancelling his £700-a-week, five-year contract signed in January that year. Dee wasn't surprised: 'I often had trouble keeping awake for the show myself. People don't want to stay up all hours on a Sunday night. They have to get up early for work the next day.' The break-up with London Weekend was acrimonious, Programming Head Stella Richman accusing him of conceit and arrogance. With aspirations to be an actor some critics felt that he suffered from the actors 'disease', that of insecurity, and that he lived under the fear that the bubble of his career was about to burst. Small roles in *The Italian Job* as a Savile Row outfitter, Mr Fish, and as Basil Beauchamp in *Doctor in Trouble* fulfilled his thespian cravings: 'TV has been good to me. I know that but everything I've done has been on the fringes of what I really wanted to do, to act.' His fall from grace was played out unceasingly in the public eye as he switched to a short-lived slot on Radio Four's *Today* and was promptly dismissed after an interview about accidents on motorways: 'Let's build barriers on them now, start Monday, stop more people getting killed'. His continued use of the word peace during his diatribes also didn't help.

Journalists anxious to speak to the former golden boy after the dust settled were greeted on his answerphone with the message, 'Thank you very much for calling and, even if you don't leave a message, thank you for the thought, peace.' The *Daily Mirror*'s top showbiz journalist, Donald Zec, tracked him down at the end of 1970 to discover he had not been idle. He had been working for Shelter, delivered a petition to Prime Minister Edward Heath at 10 Downing Street to stop the sale of arms to South Africa and walked out (in true Dee style) on a series of projected ads for a washing-up liquid. He spoke to Zec at his elegant West London flat with its large tank of tropical fish underneath a poster of Harold Wilson transposed on to the shoulders of Mao Tse-Tung. Three and a half million had been produced for the recent general election with help from Dee. He claimed the Special Branch were still after him for that stunt but 'I don't give a shit'. He still had plans to get back into chat: 'Mao Tse-Tung, I'd like to get him on television and ask him pointedly, "What do you think of me, Mao?" But nobody wants that sort of thing'.

December 1970 saw him signing on the dole. The *Daily Sketch* joined him for a trip to open a pet shop in Richmond, for the princely sum of £25. The owner assured Dee that the police had warned him about controlling the crowd expected for the opening but only seven people turned up. Dee had a stern rebuke for a photographer who startled the macaws with his flash gun: 'They're not used to that in the jungle. Try to have some sense will you'. Autographs were signed 'Peace – Simon Dee'. In 1971 ATV devised a religious show for him called *Thou Shalt Not* where he would interview personalities and host discussions on what the Ten Commandments meant to them. His request for a £100-a-week salary ensured he didn't get the job. His only weekly appearance now was well away from the public eye at Fulham Labour Exchange where he received £9 4s a week inclusive of child benefit.

> *I'm tired of being treated like a piece of Lego.*
>
> Simon Dee

In 1975 he told the *Daily Mirror*, 'I shall never use that name again, Dee no longer exists. I now call myself by my real name, Nicholas Henty-Dodd. He's the man I'd like people to listen to. He really has something to say.' Shortly after he publicly failed the test to get a job as a bus driver but was more than willing to help out in other areas: 'Britain is going through a severe economic crisis, which is getting worse because no action is being taken. I'd like to use my knowledge of television to help Britain.'

A short spell in his former occupation as a DJ with Radio 210 in Reading, brought him back to showbiz but the image was shattered once more when he faced a shoplifting charge in 1979. The incident in Woolworths, Richmond, brought him back into the news. He was found guilty and fined £25 for stealing a potato peeler and a ball. Dee claimed he had gone into the store with £36 to look at gardening equipment: 'There was nothing that caught my eye. Then I saw the name Lancashire which is where I was born, and then I saw the potato peeler. My wife had asked me to buy one, so I picked it up and put it in my pocket. I then looked at the balls for my son and bounced one, then I left the store'. He told the court, 'I often put things into my pocket before paying for them because I want my hands free.' He shouted out in court, 'I'm unable to pay. If someone will find me a job, then I'll pay.' The magistrate ordered him to pay at the rate of £1 a week.

Signing to Radio Luxembourg in 1981 to host a chat show seemed the perfect springboard back to fame but in classic Dee style he failed to turn up for the first show. 'They didn't make me the right offer. So what? Who needs them?' he told the press. A legacy of £10,000 from his grandfather in the early 1980s helped, but by 1985 the money was gone, his wife had left him with his children and he served a month's jail sentence for non-payment of rates. He made a brief appearance back on TV in *Did You See . . .?* in 1987, writing a film script.

He wrote to the *Sunday Telegraph* in April 1988 to vilify his former programme bosses at both the BBC and LWT, who he claimed in one particular incident had threatened to remove him from the screen if he mentioned President Kennedy. He also laid claim to an idea of bringing together the forces of entertainment and communication for a global TV pop show which he was told would be 'too expensive'. He claimed his idea was then adapted and the concept passed on to Bob Geldof. The letter ended with a warning: 'It may truly be said that never in our history has our youth been so violent in thought and deed. The speed with which they have, unknowingly, fallen from days of polite and organised grace has been entirely due to the mindless importing of American "junk" programmes containing endless scenes and dialogue lauding as permissible sexual, drug-orientated and violent themes.'

Two spots on *The Sound of the 60s* for Radio 2 at the close of the year saw him working for the BBC once more, for the first time in almost twenty years. He gave the press his forthright opinion on the current spate of chat shows and his own career: 'I've got my fingers crossed that this break will lead to more radio work. But TV? Forget it. It's junk. Look at what passes for talk shows. All that touching the knee stuff on *Wogan*. I won't even watch it.' Astonishingly, even for Simon Dee, after warm praise for his shows, he launched another attack on his former BBC boss in the *News of the World*. An ill-advised outing to Australia as a chat-show host ended as a flop. In 1988 he revealed that the CIA were running British television. The 1980s closed with the press reporting that both gas and his telephone had been cut off at his house. Considering that real talent is thinly spread across the myriad of television channels in the mid nineties it's incredible that no one has attempted to revive the great man's career.

MICHAEL PARKINSON

No matter how much we, who labour in television might believe that we are enabling nation to speak unto nation, and that it has significance beyond the moment, we should heed the lesson that, after a decade of interviewing the great and the good, all anyone remembers about the Parkinson *show is that the host was once savaged by a man with a fake bird on his arm.*

Michael Parkinson

In 1995 a journalist went to BBC Television Centre to interview Michael Parkinson in anticipation of the forthcoming best of *Parkinson* series. The security woman at the gate had no idea who he was as he wasn't listed in her telephone directory. Does he go under another name she pondered, perhaps Mike or Mick? In his 1970s heyday Parkinson would have swept regally into the studios but now, nearly fifteen years on, his name was greeted with a blank look. His career had never collapsed like other stars (he probably made more money in Australia in the 1980s than he ever did at the BBC) but his interviewing domination of the 'great and the good' was history, about to be dusted off for another generation to enjoy. Seeing recent repeats of Richard Burton, Orson Welles, Tommy Cooper and Peter Cook in real (not plugging-mode) conversation, with a host who clearly enjoyed their company, was a revelation to many reared on the current crop of chat shows.

Michael Parkinson is the personification of the North of England. Perennial guest Peter Cook regularly laid bets with friends on the unlikely event of a *Parkinson* show where the host didn't mention his roots. His father, a miner, was determined that his son would not follow in his footsteps but would break away from the slavery and grime of the colliery and use his talents elsewhere. He is always being accused of being a professional northerner but he has remained true to his working-class origins. In the 1970s when the *Parkinson* show was at its peak, writer Ray Connolly journeyed north with him by train to a football match. On the train he was feted by everyone much like the Hollywood film stars he interviewed. Everyone from the guard to the buffet-car staff came to pay homage to the man from Barnsley who began his career as a journalist on his local newspaper.

Parkinson spent National Service as an Army press officer and during the Suez crisis he had the unique experience of being banned from all ships of the Royal Navy after an acrimonious run-in with a group of naval officers. His first involvement in television was a major success. The Granada regional news magazine *Scene For Granada* wiped out the BBC opposition completely, its content being perfectly attuned to viewers in the north. The show is enshrined in the annals of pop music as playing host to the Beatle's first TV appearance. Indeed, when the Beatle's *Anthology* aired in 1995, the circle was completed: Granada captured the rights to the series against fierce opposition from the BBC.

Parkinson was initially a producer for the show before going in front of the cameras. He was told at his screen test it was the worst-ever performance witnessed for a Granada position. One critic at the time compared his on-screen persona to Joe Lampton from *Room at the Top*, the gritty northern hero, desperate to climb the social ladder with complete disregard for all else. *Granada in the North*, *World in Action* and *What the Papers Say* all honed his journalistic skills before joining the BBC on their flagship news programme *24 Hours*. He returned to Granada to write and host *Cinema* where his love for Hollywood and its history found full expression. An afternoon chat show, *Tea Break*, which opened with a shot of a teapot and a plate of biscuits, focused on female topics and was presented with his wife Mary. It provided a solid training ground for his future career.

Chris Kenworthy noted in the *Sun* in September 1970 with great foresight, 'One of the great mysteries of television is that nobody has managed to persuade, cajole, bully, bribe or blackmail Michael Parkinson into hosting a late-night chat programme.' When the BBC approached him with the idea for *Parkinson* they were astounded at how little Granada paid him, just £120 to write and present *Cinema*. He instantly impressed BBC bosses with his forthright honesty and deep knowledge of sport and film. Rather than invent an inflated salary he bluntly outlined the pittance he earned, establishing his reputation for a no-nonsense approach. He glady accepted a £20,000 salary; 'I'm rather proud of the money I earn as a measure of what I can do,' he said.

> *We always depended on the plug. Do you think Bing Crosby would give me his time just for the pleasure of my company? Bullshit.*
>
> Michael Parkinson

Parkinson began life as a series of eight shows in the summer of 1971. Three hundred and sixty-one shows and 1050 interviews later, Parkinson had 'sat next to most of my heroes, inspected some of the world's best hairpieces and been mugged by an emu'. Show one featured Arthur Askey and Terry-Thomas and included Royal paparizzi specialist Ray Bellasario, defending himself against a member of the League of Empire Loyalists. Recorded a few hours before transmission on Saturday night it allowed for bleeping unsavoury words but not a full editing process. This step into Frost territory was never repeated.

The production team had great difficulty in the early days landing really big names. The attitude of every agent of a major star was to wait and see how the series progressed. Orson Welles' appearance was their big breakthrough. Although the caprices of the famous, it was agreed, would not be tolerated, Parkinson's producer flew to Spain to meet up with Welles who was filming a sherry commercial. He agreed to do the show on the lure of two first-class seats on British Airways. He then only agreed to fly if the seats were removed so he could lie down in the cabin. When he boarded the plane he ignored the gap and sat somewhere else. As Parkinson explained, it was a matter of jumping through hoops just to get that first big guest.

After the appearance of Welles, agents rang the BBC to get their clients on the show. Otherwise his production team approached agents and told them they would not bow to any demands placed on them. The BBC flexed its muscles for anyone not prepared to toe the line: it was the top-rated show of the day and was big enough to quash the whims of anyone who made conditions on their appearance. One rule made from day one was that the show would never leave Television Centre, the guests always had to travel there. The host would never go cloth cap in hand in search of stars no matter who they were and this remained the standard throughout all the series. *Parkinson* suffered from as much relentless plugging as any contemporary chat show but the host succeeded in accepting it and then doing his level best to dispose of the subject at the very beginning of the interview or build it into the chat seamlessly.

Parkinson laid down the ground-rules early on when several swear words from Peter O'Toole were bleeped by the BBC before transmission (indeed Muhammad Ali was bleeped years later, not for swearing but for singing the 'Ovaltine Song', and transgressing the BBC's strict advertising rules). Parkinson told the press, 'I'd rather have Peter O'Toole and get a few laughs than be all worthwhile and bore the pants off everybody.' An early lesson was learnt by the host when actors Donald Sutherland and Elliott Gould appeared. Appearing tired and emotional they resisted all the efforts of Parkinson to speak about any subject. In desperation the host asked them if they were keen on cricket, only to be met with even blanker looks. TV critic Richard Last aptly summed them up as one, dark and inarticulate and the other, fair and inarticulate. He felt that Parkinson had fallen into the trap that had awaited Eamonn Andrews on his show, that it was always widely felt on television that because actors are trained in delivering other people's words they must have plenty of their own. It was a mistake Parkinson would not repeat.

The show made its first big headlines with the remarkable Muhammad Ali interview in which Parkinson stood up to the heavyweight champion of the world on his strict religious views and whether a boxing critic was obliged to have been a practitioner of the art. The verbal sparring from the host outdid Ali completely who was reduced to telling Parkinson, 'You are nothing, nothing'. Clive James commented in the *Observer*, 'Parky could be forgiven for failing to articulate it. Considering that the heavyweight champion of the world was apparently about to go berserk with rage only a few feet from his nose.'

James Thomas of the *Daily Express* defined what the *Parkinson* show was all about: 'Parkinson's secret seems to be that he remains excited by the people he is interviewing. There is never a blasé moment. He has learned to listen and not butt in at the wrong moment.' Parkinson always behaved like a fan in his interviews. Be it Lauren Bacall, Henry Fonda or Fred Astaire, the star-struck host always sat back and let his guest do the talking as he gazed on with the look of a man saying, 'I really am sitting alongside one of the greatest ever Hollywood stars'. He summed up his technique thus: 'I have only one acid test, do I want to interview this person or not? It has to be personal and a very intimate business in which I have taken a great deal of trouble to find out everything about the person who is going to be in the chair. I've been criticized for being a little too irreverent but I don't think that's the point so long as the person being interviewed is at ease and can answer unusual questions without embarrassment. It's never been my idea to embarrass people. The abrasive chat show man may have his place, but I like to feel at ease with people around me. My theory about chat shows has been to let the guests talk. The audience will take care of itself. Who am I to argue with Ustinov or Travers. It's much more important if they speak for themselves.'

The most appearances on *Parkinson* were made by Peter Ustinov, the host's favourite interviewee was Dr Jacob Bronowski and the women who sat opposite he claimed he adored were Diana Rigg, Shirley MacLaine, Miss Piggy and Dame Edith Evans. Muhammad Ali was 'without doubt the most remarkable human being I ever encountered'. Barbara Woodhouse told him what to do if a dog was seen fouling the footpath, 'Take the nearest heavy object, like a rolled-up newspaper, and give the culprit a hefty smack on the head.' 'Hit the dog!' said Parkinson, 'No silly boy the owner.' But he was not impressed with the king of the talk show, Johnny Carson; 'Carson doesn't do a talk show as such, he does this talk and variety show.' Parkinson felt that although this style was popular in the US and that Carson was a 'brilliant' stand up comic and a magnificent quick witted man', the American style did not allow for intellectual discussion or incisive questions. Parkinson was voted top male personality at the *Sun* TV Awards of 1973, replacing Cliff Richard.

> *If you peck me I'll break your neck and his bloody arm.*
> Billy Connolly to Emu and Rod Hull

The 1974 interview with Richard Burton came after the actor had spent six weeks drying out. The interview was taped early morning in case of a lapse by the star with the only audience the producers could find: the BBC kitchen staff. When Burton was confronted with the white-coated assembly he said, 'I thought I was back in that bloody clinic again.' After weeks of meetings, Peter Sellers tried to pull out of a show as he couldn't face walking down the stairs at the beginning as himself. The problem was solved when he donned a German army 'coal scuttle' helmet and launched himself into Kenneth Mars' spiel about Hitler from the film *The Producers*.

Parkinson observed of his trade: 'The strange thing about chat shows is that the critics hate them but they're loved by the public. Good telly is giving people what they want to watch, and talking heads are the very stuff of broadcasting. My strength is that I can interview anyone from W. H. Auden to Miss Piggy, because I'm genuinely interested in what they have to say. If I've got a style, it's getting to things by stealth. But if you see yourself as the star of even your own chat show you lose sight of the chat-show exercise. Your job as host is to reinforce the ego opposite you.' Parkinson was always riled with press reviews which claimed a show was boring because of the guests. 'I don't accept that if he was boring, it was my fault – I didn't bring him out.' It was alleged he kept a black book on journalists who continually knocked the programme so he could confront them if they ever crossed his path.

A vital component of the Parkinson experience was that the conversation never tailed off into silence, although he did speculate that a selection of magic tricks from the host might have entertained his audience more than some verbally challenged guests. 'If I'm calm it spreads to other people. In any case I would never deliberately discomfort one of my guests any more than I would a guest at a dinner party. The people who come on my show aren't criminals to be cross-examined. If there's anything they don't want to talk about I respect that area of privacy but I don't shrink from my duty of asking pertinent questions.'

Parkinson's interview with Val Doonican exemplified his clever process of drawing out his guests and making them fully relaxed. The Irish entertainer began talking about his father and Parkinson feared the interview was heading down a blind alley, the subject of a loving parent potentially a turn-off for the viewing millions. In the end Parkinson was reduced to tears along with most of the studio audience as Doonican related the final part of his father's life. 'He died of cancer of the throat. He knew that he was dying, but he didn't want my mother to know, or any of us. The loneliness of the whole thing really gets me – there he was down in his little hut in the garden trying to cope with it on his own. Finally, he had to go into hospital and I used to go and see him every day when I came home from school. My mother used to send him up his tobacco, matches and daily paper and I would take them to him. As time went on, his whole face disappeared into bandages, but the last thing he said to me has to be the most profound thing I have ever heard in my life: I sat by the bed talking to him and he told me that as he was going to die pretty soon, he didn't want me to come and see him any more. I got up to say goodbye to him and he told me that he had something he thought he should say to me – "You think I'm terrific don't you?" I replied that I did. "Well I think it's only fair that before I die you should know that I'm not. When I'm gone, I'm sure a lot of people will tell you that I'm no good and there is nothing that would please me more than for you to say: yes I know, he told me that himself."

In 1979 the programme became a twice-weekly affair with serious subjects and topics on Wednesday and showbiz on Saturdays. With guests of the calibre of Henry Kissinger and Lord Snowdon, the Wednesday-night show reguarly claimed over seven million viewers. During this period the show was branded as bordering on the crude with headlines appearing such as My Show's Not Mucky Storms Parky. A succession of guests such as Bernard Manning, Bette Midler and Billy Connolly had succeeded in antagonizing the moral guardian of obscenity, Mary Whitehouse. Midler had sung a song about VD and threatened to remove her dress, revelling in the fact, as she told her host, that she could never get away with material like that in her home country. Connolly had told a succession of farting jokes whilst Manning made crude remarks to the house band.

She complained, 'Lately he seems to have been positively egging on his guests to be crude, and giving them a push towards being salacious. I think ordinary people are getting fed up with this sort of thing. If it continues I think a whole lot of people will simply give up watching the Parkinson show. I know I already have.' Parkinson responded, 'The majority of people who didn't like those shows are professional complainers, and they are such a tiny population I don't think I should be governed by their views.' One of the Billy Connolly interviews in question summed up the divide between UK chat shows and US. When he mentioned during a story that he had been 'as welcome as a fart in a space-suit', fellow guest, US actress Angie Dickinson broke up hysterically, aware that this sort of humour would never get past the TV networks in her own country.

During this period the BBC board of governors convened to discuss extending the show US-style to five nights a week but the idea was shelved. Parkinson was enamoured by the idea after watching a *Tonight Show* when Carson ran out of time to interview Count Basie but invited him back the following night. However he faced more than the decision of the BBC governors. NUJ members at the BBC voted the idea down provoking 42 Labour MP's to table a House of Commons motion against it.

In 1981, London Weekend decided to take on *Parkinson* by running old Johnny Carson *Tonight Shows* against him. The BBC reacted quickly and moved Parkinson back to the 9.35 PM slot before *Match of the Day*. He was justly angry that ITV lacked the imagination to produce their own chat show and utilize home-grown talent rather than the man who was responsible for over a third of NBC's profits: 'There is no way Carson is ever going to work in Britain. So all the viewers will get are second-hand shows.' Ironically Parkinson was on holiday in California and attending a Carson taping when news of the ITV sale was announced. With his wife sitting next to him he was amongst audience members used for reaction shots to the news. (At the time Parkinson was also proud of the fact that Robert Redford had appeared on his show but had never graced the *Tonight Show*.)

'Carson's brain is so tuned into the American culture, so excessively American that you'd need to give him a lobotomy for him to work here. If Michael Grade (then head of LWT) is seriously telling me that there is no one in this country who could fill that slot better than Carson, then as a shareholder of LWT I have got one or two questions I want to ask him. It is a privilege for anyone to have an hour of TV time at their disposal and to give it a rehash of an American show is a sign of desperation. I would rather see anybody up against me than this. Why don't they just give some youngster a chance in this country. I mean God almighty if the BBC's Bill Cotton hadn't given me a chance eleven years ago, where would I be now.' Parkinson was proved right in the end when LWT's transmission of the *Tonight Show* was cancelled early on. No attempt has been made since to broadcast the show on terresterial television.

> *When we first met, he looked in despair at the sheet of paper I*
> *had in my hand. 'What is that?' he said. My questions I said.*
> *'Throw them away and we will talk instead, much better,'*
> *he said. And it was.*
>
> Michael Parkinson on Orson Welles

The *Parkinson* series finished for good on 3 April 1982, as the host got ready to set up TV-AM and expand his interviewing horizons to Australia. The final guest line-up was the Parky dream team of Billy Connolly, Spike Milligan, Kenneth Williams and Jimmy Tarbuck. Milligan closed the proceedings with a custard pie in the face of the host.

> *The best talk show of all time.*
>
> Spike Milligan

Many in the business felt that by this time he had completely lost interest in the subjects he interviewed. He admitted the last series had been on auto-pilot and he should have taken a year off. He had interviewed all the top names in the seventies and had nothing left to prove. Parkinson had every right to be proud of the fact that in his estimation less than 40 per cent of the guests on the show had been there to plug something, the rest where there simply to chat, now a real rarity. He has little time for today's chat shows: 'People say the show I did in the seventies was better because nowadays the agents rule the talk shows and tell the host what he can say and what he can't. Well, that's always been the case. What's changed is the craven manner in which people now accept that bollocks.'

There was a very brief flirtation with the US when he hosted two Dick Cavett shows but hated the ratings-obsessed world of US television. The formula in Australia was an instant hit where he was labelled 'the thinking woman's crumpet'. Parky parties were all the rage when friends gathered together to watch the show. His million-pound contract was a far cry from his first wage packet from the BBC as a chat-show host.

He returned to British screens in March 1987 with *Parkinson One to One* for ITV. It was the classic *Parkinson* format, 45 minutes spent in the company of one guest, drawn from a wide range, Jack Lemmon to Ian Botham. Mark Lawson of the *Independent* hailed the triumphant return: 'Parkinson remains the best chat-show host we have: it may be a small honour (like being the tallest dwarf) but it is something.' A second series delivered a further batch of guests of the stature of Anthony Hopkins, Phil Collins and Cliff Richard. Parkinson recognised his elevation beyond the mere mortals of the chat-show world: 'This kind of show is the only thing that interests me now. Going back to three on a couch holds no interest for me at present. One to one was always my favourite form of interview, you have got to be prepared to play second fiddle. I don't like interviewers who intrude. I think people who butt in, or have to involve showgirls are disguising a sloppy approach. Your job as an interviewer is to be the medium through which the audience meets the guests. You are not there to show what a pretty person you are.' Desmond Morris analysed the success of Parkinson by exploring his body language: he claimed the host projected the aura of someone performing a natural act in unnatural surroundings.

The ITV series wrapped due to a lack of guests of sufficient star quality. When Peter Sellers and Dame Edith Evans died their appearances on the *Parkinson* show were used as tributes. In 1989 Parkinson admitted, 'I am bored with the chat-show format which I have been doing for the past twenty years.' Parkinson began to hack out a new career on *Give Us a Clue, All Star Secrets, Desert Island Discs, The Help Squad* and *Going For a Song.*

> *Until then, a very good night. Goodnight.*
> Michael Parkinson

In 1995 the BBC launched a summer season of great interviews from the series hosted by the star. Most critics agreed the format had worn well alongside the host despite some of the shows being almost 25 years old. Tim De Lisle in the *Independent*: 'Today's Parky re-appeared to sum up. A proud sadness in his baggy eyes suggested a man in mourning not just for his guest (Peter Cook) but for his genre.' Lynne Truss in *The Times*: 'Looking back, the extraordinary and innocent thing about Parkinson was his genuine admiration for the people he interviewed, and his frequent beetroot-faced appearance of a man being tickled to death when they told funny stories. In his reaction shots during Niven's anecdotes his face swelled to bursting with unexpressed laughter as though plugged at the mouth with a towel. Parkinson described his seventies appearance: 'I'm wearing these extraordinary, bloody great big collars and I've got the sort of hair that wasn't sideboards but joined at the bottom like a hairy balaclava.' His legendary mannerisms he insisted were a sign that he was completely relaxed.

The name Parkinson has become synonymous in this country with chat and his surname alone is enough to conjure instant nostalgia for television in the 1970s and the stellar collection of stars he interviewed. Ironically, after the success of the 'best of series' plans are now in hand to relaunch the show. It's almost akin to Kevin Keegan returning now to the England team or Donny Osmond topping the chart again. With such a paucity of interviewing talent around the master is returning to show everyone how it should be done.

RUSSELL HARTY

You have, have you not . . .?

Russell Harty

Russell Harty's route into television chat stardom is probably
the strangest and certainly the boldest in this book. The son
of a fruit and vegetable stallholder and a former housemaster
at Giggleswick School, he returned in 1967 from a period as
lecturer in English Literature at City University, New York, and
answered an advert to become an arts producer on Radio 3.
He produced *The World of Books, The Critics Choice of Paperbacks*
and originated *The Arts This Week*. He soon progressed to the
fledgeling ITV network London Weekend (part-owned by David
Frost) where he became involved with Humphrey Burton who
produced a late-night arts strand. He won an Emmy (TV's Oscars)
for his stunningly realized documentary on the surrealist painter
Salvador Dali which encompassed many elements of his work,
delving into his fantasy world. He also won a Golden Harp for
his documentary on the Finnian Games, Scotland's traditional
highland games.

His progression to chat show was easily accomplished: he
convinced London Weekend controller Cyril Bennett he would
be the perfect anchorman for a US-style chat show. Alan
Bennett saw his unique interviewing style as 'untouched by

expertise'. His trademark interview style – camp, raised eyebrow, arch manner and elongated Lancastrian vowels – was that of a neighbour chatting over the fence; but this was the deceptive front of a deeply cerebral man. He was the complete opposite to his chat-show contemporary Michael Parkinson who projected a bluff, assertive, virile style. Both men, however, were great friends, sharing a common love of the North of England, its traditions, Gracie Fields and Hilda Ogden.

The show hit the headlines early on when in an interview with the Who both him and the group stripped off and carried on talking. Harty claimed that with his show, 'It's the closest thing to Horlicks. It warms you up, gives you a good feeling and after you watch me, you toddle off to bed for a nice deep sleep.' An Old Bailey secrets trial was halted after comments by a guest on the show. *Russell Harty Plus*, *Saturday Night People*, *Russell Harty* and *Harty* all became mainstays for Independent Television throughout the 1970s. *Saturday Night People* was a short-lived variation hosted by Harty, Clive James and Janet Street-Porter, to provide sophisticated bitchy entertainment. He was awarded the Royal Television Society's Most Oustanding Male Newcomer award in 1973 and featured in *Harty Welcome* and *Behave Yourself* before making the switch to BBC. He replaced Desmond Wilcox on the Radio 4 chat show *Midweek* and proved even more accomplished at interviewing on radio than on TV.

> *I feel like I've gone from a corner shop to Tescos.*
> Russell Harty

When he joined the BBC in 1980 on a £50,000-a-year contract he reached a national audience for the first time, his ITV shows never being fully networked. He joined the BBC as a natural replacement for Michael Parkinson who had left to set up TV-AM. Within a few weeks of the show's launch the incident occurred with Grace Jones that would haunt him ever after. After performing 'Private Life' the model-turned-dance-diva was interviewed but it soon became clear she was not giving sensible answers to Harty's questions. Producer Tom Gutteridge told Harty through his earpiece to move swiftly on to the next guest, Royal photographer Patrick Lichfield. Jones became angry that her interview had been truncated and began interrupting. At one point she fell off her seat and her speech became slurred. She told Harty, 'I don't like being ignored, nor do I like your back turned on me. I've had enough – I'm leaving now.' Harty asked her to remain in her seat and said he would talk to her shortly. As he turned back to his other guest he was hit by a rain of blows from Jones and had to cover his head to protect his face and body from the punches.

He said after the show, 'All creatures are flesh and blood and people have different ways of expressing themselves. This apparently was hers.' The classic piece of footage is still used on BBC directors' courses as the prime example of how not to arrange chairs for guests on a chat show (so that the presenter has to turn his back on a guest). The revised and all-improved 'Harty Semi-Circle' was utilized for *Wogan* and when Harty was told of this development he surmised this would probably be recognised as his greatest contribution to broadcasting.

Like his sojourn with ITV there was a stable of programmes utilizing his surname, *With Russell Harty* and *Harty at the Seaside*. He also took over Roy Plomley's radio classic *Desert Island Discs* and manufactured a TV version. His Tuesday and Thursday night BBC2 slot provided a full week of chat for the corporation with Terry Wogan on Monday, Wednesday and Friday. But he bore no ignominy when Wogan landed the plum job: 'I didn't feel to deposed when Terry Wogan was given three nights a week. I was quite happy to move aside. I know that I am not the world's most popular broadcaster. I'm much too strange. Wogan is fiendishly popular. I have never attained or aspired to that level of popularity. All I want to do is work.'

A summer special at Blackpool showed his caring side when he asked his audience if everybody was enjoying themselves. A tearful woman replied she wasn't, as her husband had recently died. As the cameras kept rolling Harty consoled the tearful woman, restoring her spirits. His easy-going demeanour disguised an ability to upset guests which revealed itself to Danny Kaye, Rita Hayworth, Angela Lansbury (questioned on her corns) and David Bowie, who was asked why he appealed to men as much as women. As Harty said, 'I don't like making enemies but I can be difficult and bitchy if I want. It depends how I feel at the time.' When conversation lagged with Arnold Schwarzenegger, he asked him, 'Tell us something interesting.' The beefy actor replied, 'I bought a cashmere sweater yesterday.' His 1982 Christmas Eve show *Chez Harty* was a ratings winner for BBC2. Harty chatted with guests at his Giggleswick cottage, interrupted by carols and general festive bonhomie. His only worry, he confessed to a journalist, was whether he 'put another log on the fire too ostentatiously'. By 1983 the *Sun* had crowned him king of chat. His formula was simple: 'A TV studio is the falsest, silliest surrounding to have a laid-back conversation in front of three million people.' Guests were told, 'Don't mind about the audience, just tell me.' He claimed, 'The secret is . . . there's no secret. It's actually a question of getting used to the machinery. The moment you realize you needn't pretend, you move on.'

He took his chat show to the streets of Widnes in 1983, randomly calling at houses for 'a cup of tea and a natter'. One woman told him she was too busy and shut the door on him whilst another, when asked if the kettle was on, replied no and said she was going out. The next day, a newspaper reporter tried the same trick at the Harty household and was rewarded with a cup of tea from Harty's PA but a disinclination from the TV star for a 'natter'. He famously induced Margaret Thatcher to reveal her favourite snack, poached eggs on Bovril smeared toast. In 1988 he made *Mr Harty's Grand Tour*, a four-part travelogue in which, with quintessential Harty style, he asked former Hitler associate Lady Diana Mosley whether the dictator had good manners. He also formed the British League for Hilda Ogden with Sir John Betjeman, Willis Hall and Michael Parkinson.

His latter years had been the subject of extensive hounding by the tabloid press over the nature of his long hospitalization. His broadcasting career had ended shortly before when he hosted Radio 4's *Start the Week*. He died on June 8th of hepatitis and liver failure, hounded by the press until the end, all desperate to get a picture of him in his hospital bed.

The *Independent* defined him as a man who was able to chat to prime ministers, popes and Blackburn pensioners in much the same manner. Michael Parkinson delivered the eulogy at a service for Harty at Blackburn Cathedral. Harty's biggest fear about his obituary was that it would be headed Grace Jones Man Dead. When both men had attended a Gracie Fields memorial service, Russell had struck a deal: 'If I do yours, will you do mine. You can tell them about Grace Jones and I'll tell them about the emu.'

DAVID LETTERMAN

'What's the difference between Bernard Manning and David Letterman? David Letterman gets paid more! Has the transmission of David Letterman In London been a deliberate ploy to make us realise what it is like to be racially abused in our own country? Bernard Manning is pilloried for making racist comments as part of his stage show. The first half of David Letterman's show was nothing more than a succession of "jokes" which were all variations on a theme. One evening he wheeled on a "London town crier" to proclaim "I'm knackered" – a joke Letterman had been running throughout the programme. We had funny policemen, a guardsman in his sentry box as an Aunt Sally, Zsa Zsa Gabor regurgitating jellied eels and, of course, Royal Family jokes. Would, say, Bob Monkhouse be allowed into America to do a show focusing on Bill Clinton and his family? On their adaption of the English language? Or am I just being sensitive? No, I was being offered abuse in the name of humour. How dare BBC2 and satellite allow this man ten hours of screen time for his self-indulgent, abusive show. Will the PM please make a statement in the House? And will this man get back to where he belongs. (Now where have I heard that before.)'

David Watson, Huntingdon
Letter to Radio Times, *June 1995*

'Has the BBC now taken to handing out drugs or other artificial stimulants to studio audiences prior to recording or transmission? I ask because the audience behaviour on David Letterman In London beggars belief. Whooping, whistling, cheers, applause out of all proportion to the mediocre inanities presented (often performed hands overhead, just to make sure), and a climate of hysterical adulation, made me wonder if they and I were watching the same programme! A more mundane, lacklustre talk show would be hard to imagine (and let's not forget, Letterman is competing with some real home-grown dross in this field), and yes, it seems, if people cheer and applaud long enough and loud enough, they'll kid themselves into thinking they're having a good time. It was an utterly embarrassing and sorry spectacle.'

Dave Godin, Sheffield
Letter to Radio Times, *June 1995*

America has produced two chat hosts who have refined the genre and elevated it to an art. Johnny Carson is the master and David Letterman his protégé. Letterman has always stated that Carson is his bench-mark in all that he does. Hotly tipped to take over the *Tonight Show* in 1992, he was bitterly disappointed when Jay Leno was awarded the hottest seat in US showbiz. Letterman's show *Late Night with Letterman* is the epitome of East-Coast hipness with its stylish host, guests and inspired comedy. When the BBC decided to devote a week to the show, when it was broadcast from London, the reaction amongst British viewers was indignant, as defined by the spluttering letters to the *Radio Times* reproduced above. Americans are very different from the English and none more so than in the world of chat shows.

Terry Wogan appeared to rapturous applause but the audience soon settled in their seats and were quiet enough for all kind of backstage noises to be heard. When Letterman walks on stage each night at the Ed Sullivan Theatre on Broadway he has to strive hard to make the audience settle down as a tumult of whooping and applause rocks the theatre's foundations.

Letterman is famed for setting the theatre air conditioning almost at freezing to keep his audience alert and hungry for more guests and gags.

Being a guest on *Letterman* is no easy road. If someone decides to sit back on the show and offer little input, the cranky host will go for the jugular. Jerry Seinfeld, one of America's top comedians was recently being fed questions by Letterman so he could fire back, apparently off-the-cuff humour. But no name is too great for Letterman to sabotage and slowly the conversation was led on to subjects that weren't in the comedian's brief and Seinfeld struggled to ad-lib. As Robert MacKenzie observed in *TV Guide*, 'If guests start to drown on this show, they get little help from the host. He'll not only sit there and watch them go down, but he's apt to toss them an iron life-jacket.' Letterman rides it all out with a wry smile, unfailingly polite, but the point has been made. Producer Barry Sand claims, 'He is one of the greatest ad-libbers who ever lived. He comes back with a quip that you couldn't write in a million years.'

Accused of being 'condescending, smug, even mean', Letterman replies, 'I suppose I am all of those things, but we never invite somebody on to demonstrate condescension – or condensation. If somebody comes on and is a bonehead and is loafing through an interview, I resent that, and maybe I will go after them. I'm stunned at the number of people in showbusiness who come and don't seem to get what we want from them is a performance.' Letterman's most famous interview, with Madonna in March 1995, was certainly a performance. She had long been the butt of many jokes on the programme and the interview for her was payback time. As she chomped on a cigar and delivered a stream of obscenities Letterman fired back a volley of one-liners which brought him total empathy from the audience and kept him firmly in the driving seat. The interview made news across the world but the two were later reconciled as presenters at the MTV Awards.

David certainly had a wacky sense of humour.
Sidney Maurer, owner of Atlas Supermarket

Letterman was born in Indianapolis, Indiana, and was brought up on the television of the 1950s. He worshipped Steve Allen, Jonathan Winters and of course Johnny Carson, then a game-show host. His road to fame was launched in a public speaking class. By his own admission he did not shine at other subjects but emoting to an audience presented no problems: 'For the first time in my formal academic experience there was a subject that seemed to come easily to me, more easily than algebra or geometry or shop. I was not very bright, and may not be very bright in the rest of my life, but at that time it was clear to me that this was something to remember. That this was a valuable lesson.' A three-year term as a supermarket bagger at the Atlas Supermarket after school gave him a lifelong interest in packing and every year *Late Night* features America's champion grocery bagger as a nod to its host first job. At the supermarket he regularly caused chaos. He would get customers to write their names on receipts and put them in a box for a grand prize draw for a non-existent car. Or he would fill empty cornflake boxes with corn husks and put them on the shelves causing consternation amongst customers.

He majored in media studies at Ball State University, Muncie, Indiana (where he married his college sweetheart Michelle Cook) and experienced broadcasting for the first time on the college radio station and later got a job at his local station WERK. In true Letterman style he funded a scholarship in communications at the college after he found television fame and also paid a substantial sum to re-equip the radio and television department. However, it was revealed in 1990 that the only students eligible for the scholarship were those with a C average, the rating that Letterman under-achieved in his college days. A plaque on the wall of the studio facility funded by Letterman bears the inscription, 'Dedicated to all the C students before and after me. Signed David M. Letterman'.

Here I was at nineteen, talking to central Indiana. Of course,
central Indiana wasn't listening.

David Letterman

In 1968 he became an underling at his local TV station, WLWI-TV Channel 13, where he gave out the station's call sign every half hour and announced public service messages. This vacation job became full-time on leaving college and he stayed with the station for five years learning almost every facet of broadcasting. His early years consisted of three main jobs. Substitute weatherman on weekend news programmes, interviewer on a Saturday afternoon kids show and host of the late-night movie (a slot he renamed 'Freeze-Dried Movies'). Although he enjoyed utilizing his anarchic humour with kids and late-night film viewers, his weather forecasts were in a class of their own. He would tell viewers, 'Nothing is going to happen to us as far as weather is concerned. It's going to be just like it was yesterday, and just like it is today, and it's going to be like that tomorrow and again on Tuesday, because nothing's going on.' Hailstones were falling like 'cans of ham' and storms were given standing ovations when they were upgraded by the US weather service to hurricanes. Viewers were told that Indiana and Ohio had merged into one large state or that Georgia had been removed from the map and replaced by Iran and its population.

Determined not to be tied to local television for the rest of his career, in 1974 Letterman auditioned for WNTS radio in Indianapolis and gained a presenting job as host on a phone-in show and as the drive-time jock. It was short-lived, as Letterman explained: 'I hated it. I was miscast because you have to be somebody who is fairly knowledgeable, fairly glib, possessing a natural interest in a number of topics. That certainly is not me, I don't care about politics, I don't care about the world economy, I don't care about Martians cleaning our teeth. The Nixon–Watergate nonsense was the perfect example of something about which I knew nothing and couldn't have cared less. All I wanted to do was get home at the end of the day and drink beer. In the meantime, all these political mavens would call wanting to discuss the intricacies of the left and the right and what did I know? I was just your average jerk, so I didn't do them much good. I did it for a year and literally thought I would lose my mind. This was around the time of Watergate, and most of our callers thought homosexuals and people from Jupiter were behind it all.'

The boredom led to Letterman indulging in practical jokes once more. He told Indianapolis residents that the focal point of the city, the 230-foot-tall Soldier's Monument, had been sold to the island of Guam, whose government planned to paint it green to honour their national vegetable, the asparagus. Despite the tedium of conducting phone-ins Letterman refined his interviewing style using the callers as comic stooges. If they couldn't be manipulated for laughs they were swiftly cut off usually with the pay-off, 'This caller must be from Mars'.

By 1976, with his career still going nowhere, he made the move that almost every US TV and film star has made, the move west to Los Angeles. His wife supported him completely but he admitted later there was one thought on his mind: 'I knew I was going to fail.' Renting a pickup truck he and his wife loaded all their worldly goods on board and set off armed with a selection of sitcom scripts. These were rejected everywhere. As he told *Playboy*, 'I told everyone, including myself, that I was going out there to become a TV scriptwriter. I thought that would be my best entry point into the business. But the thing you discover is that you can write all the scripts you want when you're living in Indianapolis. People aren't going to meet you at the L.A. city line saying, "Can we see those scripts? We're dying to get scripts from people who live in Indianapolis". It just doesn't work that way. I'd take my scripts around and they'd toss them into a warehouse, and every Thursday, the guy with the forklift would go by, pick up all the scripts and bury them near the river.'

He switched to comedy stand-up at the Comedy Store alongside the fledgeling Jay Leno and began to carve a career: 'I'd never performed as a stand-up comedian before, partly because there's just no place to do that in Indianapolis or Ball State. Oh you can do it in your home but it gets little response.' He polished his observational act and soon turned professional but admitted he didn't enjoy performing: 'I envy comedians who can go out and enjoy being in front of people. It's still something of a traumatic thing for me.' After two years of little success, his marriage foundered as he became more obsessed with achieving his showbiz goal. He wrote jokes for the comedian J. J. Walker, star of the black sitcom *Good Times,* for which he was paid $150 a week for fifteen jokes. He also wrote comic material for John Denver and Bob Hope. He was an audience warm-up man on the *Barney Miller Show* and appeared as a comedian on *The Gong Show* and Don Kirshner's *Rock Concert.* He also became a regular on the current affairs spoof *The Peeping Times.* In 1977 he gained his first starring slot on *The Starland Vocal Band Show* (a one-hit wonder band who were enjoying their fifteen minutes of fame with 'Afternoon Delight'). He appeared in comedy sketches which he also helped to write. The book *Bad TV* by Craig Nelson defines the series as 'the show that asks the question, How did you get this job?'

In 1978 he was a cast member (alongside Michael Keaton) for the all-singing, all-dancing variety series *Mary* which starred Mary Tyler Moore. As *Bad TV* also notes, 'This show was so terrible, you never saw it; of sixteen shows produced only three were aired, the whole fiasco costing CBS around $5 million.' Letterman played a wisecracking announcer, acting as a foil for Mary Tyler Moore's sweet-girl personality. It was a role he hated – the show's Mr Strait-Laced who Mary forced into song and dance numbers. It was on this show that Letterman first worked professionally with fellow writer Merrill Markoe who would become the instigator of many of the key parts of *Late Night with Letterman*. They had met before at the Comedy Store and soon also became romantically involved. She acted as his guardian angel on the show, editing out scripts and costumes that she knew would cause him embarrassment.

Despite the shows disastrous ratings, talent scouts for the *Tonight Show* noticed Letterman and he made a guest appearance with his hero Johnny Carson in November 1978. The highest accolade for a comedian on the show was to be called over to the chair next to Johnny's at the end of their act and Letterman succeeded first time out. It was generally agreed in the comedy world that Letterman had made one of the strongest *Tonight Show* debuts ever. This in turn led to a stint as a guest host, after just two more appearances, where Letterman discovered his true vocation in showbusiness. He was an instant hit with viewers and sat in the host seat more than twenty times in the next few years. His Midwestern origins mutual with Carson gave him a unique edge as he explained: 'I guess you don't expect a guy from that part of the country, someone who looks like you and me, to be clever or tricky. It's a different image than the stereotype America has of comics, guys in shiny suits telling jokes about their wives being fat.'

Letterman was soon being hailed as the number one contender for the *Tonight Show* hot seat whenever Carson decided to hang up his microphone. He appeared as a panellist on *The Gong Show* and a celebrity contestant on *The Twenty Thousand Dollar Pyramid*. He also appeared in an episode of *Mork and Mindy* as the leader of a strange cult. This acting period of his career proved to be short-lived and his appearance with Robin Williams has never been mentioned in any Letterman interviews. He is also rumoured to have appeared as a sleazy Hollywood agent in an episode of *Laverne & Shirley*. He capped his acting streak in 1979 when he appeared in a TV movie, *Fast Friends*, based around the drama of producing a daily talk show. Ironically, in the film Dick Shawn played a chat-show host who drops dead and is replaced by Letterman. A comedy series *Leave It to Dave* was abandoned after the pilot (Letterman interviewed guests, sat around him on pillows, from a throne on a set designed like the interior of a pyramid). He did a screen test for the lead in *Airplane!* (which eventually went to Robert Hays) and used this as a recommendation for anyone thinking of casting him again as a good reason not to.

After he found fame Disney signed him to a contract as an actor but nothing was ever produced. Letterman has turned up lately making small appearances in the *Bonnie Hunt Show* (produced by his company) and playing himself on the *Larry Sanders Show*. Fortune smiled on Letterman once more when NBC President Fred Silverman found himself desperate to recruit an NBC celebrity to host a charity dinner. Johnny Carson and Bill Cosby were unavailable but Letterman was. He was a knockout and Silverman vowed that he would find a vehicle for Letterman on the station.

He gained his own talk show with NBC in 1980. The show made news before it had even aired when two producers quit days before its debut (one, claimed Letterman, made rehearsal shows look like they were shot on a security camera at 7-Eleven). Merrill Markoe took up the reins and the foundations of the Letterman style began to be laid. Debuting on 23 June 1980, the *David Letterman Show* held a live 90-minute slot each day at 10 a.m. with the host defining his wacky view of life. The first show saw Letterman announce that he had been a former guest on the *Tonight Show* with the rider, 'But let's face it, who hasn't?' He made straight for the audience and asked a member of it to pop out of the studio and get him a coffee, duly tipping him on his return. The audience were made aware of his favourite request in a restaurant, 'More parsley please', and TV critic Jeff Greenfield came on to review the show while it was still on the air.

The short-lived, five-month series laid the foundations for the Letterman brand name. He would disappear from the set and let an audience member take over the hot seat or send one of their number out for a take-away (a beloved stunt which is still a regular part of *Late Night*). Excursions from the studio were commonplace as the host set out on jaunts through the New York neighbourhood in search of fun. Nobody working on the show knew where to find cue cards so they used large pieces of cardboard and felt tips. In all it was a completely shambolic exercise but it worked. The ratings however were dire and major NBC affiliates began dropping the show. David Frost and Mike Douglas producer Barry Sand was brought in to make changes. He dumped the repertory troupe who performed sketches on the show, freeing the writers to concentrate solely on Letterman and most importantly introduced ex-Jack Paar director Hal Gurnee who would become the mainstay of *Late Night* when it launched.

The show was cut to 60 minutes (Carson sent Letterman a telegram claiming, 'It took you two months to do what it took me seventeen years to do'). but this new angle on daytime US TV was doomed. The final frenetic weeks saw Letterman produce a TV on his desk and flip through the opposition channels to see what was on or ask members of the audience to take ink-blot tests to see who they would vote for and then on the basis of the results have them hauled away by men in white coats. Staples of *Late Night*, Stupid Pet Tricks and Letterman making the phone call that audience members couldn't, were all introduced. Under the threat of the axe the show became tighter and ratings began to climb but previous figures had sealed the show's fate. Despite its relative failure the show won two Emmys. Critic Tony Schwartz of the *New York Times* was prescient when he said, 'Letterman afficionados should be able to argue a case study in faulty scheduling. It is hard to imagine that there is not an audience, probably not housewives and perhaps late night, for a talk show host whom critics have called one of the cleverest, quickest and least predictable comedians around.'

NBC however were impressed by the Letterman style and he was placed on a $1 million-a-year contract to sit tight and await

The king of late night, Johnny Carson, celebrating
his twenty-second year as host of
The Tonight Show. (© NBC)

David Frost in 1962
searching for material for
*That Was The Week That
Was.* (Hulton Getty)

Eamonn Andrews leads an all-star knees up in
Piccadilly in the autumn of 1967 as ITV promotes
its new season of programmes. (Hulton Getty)

(Left) 'The BBC dictated to me. They never let me
do what I wanted.' Simon Dee joins the opposition
on 6 November 1969. (Hulton Getty)

The classic image of Michael Parkinson, suave and sophisticated, concealing his intense journalistic nature. (Hulton Getty)

'Summit meeting for chat show hosts Eamonn Andrews, Michael Parkinson and Russell Harty. (Hulton Getty)

'I'm not a talk-show host, but I play one on TV' - David Letterman. (©NBC)

'I'd gone round sticking microphones up the noses of people at Royal Film premieres and Miss World contests until I felt I couldn't do it any longer.' Michael Aspel in April 1971 during his microphone sticking period. (Hulton Getty)

Terry Wogan and wife Helen at the height of his
Radio One popularity with the 'fight the flab'
campaign.   (Hulton Getty)

(left) Oprah Winfrey in her Oscar-nominated role as
Sofia in the Steven Spielberg film *The Color Purple.*
(© Warner Bros)

David Letterman deputizes for Johnny Carson on *The Tonight Show* in 1979 with guest and future *Tonight Show* host Jay Leno. (© NBC)

'It's a constant challenge to remain interested' - Ricki Lake. (© Columbia Tristar Televison)

the call for a format that could utilize his unique style. Gossip had it that Letterman was being groomed as Carson's successor. During a *Tonight Show* monologue about the line of succession in the White House, Carson speculated would it be Letterman, Bush, Haig, or would it be Letterman, Bush, Tip O'Neill, and then Haig. A few months later when his monologue was eliciting few laughs he said, 'Why don't I just go on home and we can bring Letterman in right now.' With only one nineteen-week headlining show to his name it appeared that Letterman was almost ready to take over the most powerful slot on television. Firstly however he needed another show for his talents.

> *I can't sing, dance or act. What else would I be but a talk-show host?*
>
> David Letterman

He didn't have to wait too long. His old mentor Johnny Carson cut back the *Tonight Show* from 90 minutes to 60 leaving NBC with a vacuum in their schedule at 12.30 a.m. A current affairs programme, the *Tomorrow Show*, proved a ratings loser on the schedule and, after an attempt to boost its showbiz and comedy ratio failed, NBC decided to run with Letterman. Carson had full veto on the programme that followed his show and was more than happy to allow his Carson Productions company to produce the new show. He laid down the law on the conditions that would have to be enforced. No monologue, no more than four musicians in the house band and no sidekick on the sofa. None of this was a problem. This would be a fresh, younger idea of a late-night chat show and the need to veer away from the conservative *Tonight Show* format was essential. All of Carson's criteria were easily applied, the monologue merely re-jigged as 'opening remarks'. The old team of Merrill Markoe, Barry Sand and Hal Gurnee were brought back together, inspired by the image of Steve Allen, a man in a suit and tie surrounded by madness. *Late Night with David Letterman* filled the slot and debuted on 1 February 1982.

Its appeal was aimed at a hip suburban audience and college students, so beloved of advertisers. Letterman noted at the time, 'Our audience doesn't have to get up at eight in the morning'. As the *Complete Directory to Prime Time Network TV Shows* states, 'Late Night with David Letterman was to TV talk shows as Salvador Dali was to traditional painting'. The formula was almost identical to the *Tonight Show* but with an undercurrent of anarchy. The debut show launched with a high-kicking girl chorus and a tour backstage which featured a green room full of trees and shrubs and staff in the control room dressed in Bavarian peasant costume and singing drinking songs. Bill Murray was the very first guest, indulging himself in singing 'Let's Get Physical' and performing an aerobics routine. A trip out to the streets headlined Shame of the City exposed a delicatessen owner who had misspelt planning as 'planing' and these as 'theese' on a sign. Letterman berated him for the benefit of viewers and refused to leave until the sign was fixed. It set the tone and provided an instant empathy with the viewing audience.

Letterman could easily handle the giants of showbiz but proved himself able to interact with the public on the streets of New York in a witty way. The first show set the standard for in-your-face street confrontations that continue to this day. Critic Andrew Kopkind defined the show's appeal after its first week on air: 'Letterman is now the official host for the baby-boom culture, the audience of videonauts that laughs at sick jokes, makes sense of idiotic images and feels comfortable suspended off the wall. It's an audience that was weaned on *Mad* magazine, warmed up with recreational drugs, and trained to respond to the merest remark of Steve Martin. To these aging freaks, domesticated hippies and nostalgic iconoclasts, Carson or Cavett are not just conventional, they're incomprehensible.' The show was deemed 'hot' immediately by advertisers, attracting 'media-active' demographics not seen since the launch of *Saturday Night Live*.

The house band led by Paul Shaffer and known as The World's Most Dangerous Band were a world away from Doc

Severinsen and his jazz leanings. Master musician Shaffer led a rock band of accomplished musicians who could deliver almost any song in the vast pop canon to match the entrance of a guest. Canadian-born Shaffer headed up the band on *Saturday Night Live* before teaming up with Letterman. Aside from his musical duties Shaffer also fulfilled the second-banana role, in the style of Ed McMahon, providing a sounding board for Letterman's ruminations. Shaffer's bottomless knowledge of pop often provokes the thought 'How did he think of that?' As when Kim Basinger walked on to Prince's 'I Want to Be Your Lover', footballer Alexi Lalas to the Delfonic's 'La-La Means I Love You' or when the Top Ten Things Overheard at the Lorena Bobbitt Trial was introed by 'Everytime You Go Away' with its refrain 'You take a piece of me with you'.

Another early member of the troupe was Larry 'Bud' Melman, played by Calvert DeForest, a rotund stooge of few words who would appear as famous celebrities (in his normal persona) or roam the streets to set up gags on the public. He would wait at a New York bus station and hand hot towels to passengers arriving or stand outside the Russian Embassy and urge staff to defect with offers of domestic appliances and pornography. Head writer Merrill Markoe was responsible for instigating many of the comedy items which became a staple of the show and are still popular close on fifteen years later. Stupid Pet Tricks (first used on the daytime show) made its late-night debut with a skateboarding rabbit called Thumper. Stupid Human Tricks would later appear with, for example, a man who could pass a bean through his mouth to just below his eye socket.

An early success was the monkey-cam, where a chimpanzee had a camera secured to his head to give an ape's-eye view of the world. Another classic was something called 'the 360-degree show'. For a full hour viewers witnessed the television picture rotating very slowly, with Letterman and guests appearing upside down at the halfway point. One show was seen completely from Letterman's point of view and a Christmas special appeared in July 1982 to beat the seasonal rush. Another had the concept of dubbing the voices of all participants with British accents alongside a show filmed in reverse image. Letterman admitted he owed a debt to the past: 'We looked at some early Steve Allen shows and some really early Ernie Kovacs. One thing the shows we liked all had in common was a casual kind of liveliness, an un-slick, see the camera-cable, see the mistakes kind of things. See what we try to do is pure television. We go into the studio, use the cameras, invite the people in, we do a television show. Whereas what most other people do is produce things to be shown on television, but they're not television, they're dramas, comedies, musicals, whatever. They're at the slick end of things and we're at the bargain basement end.' Another important element which underlined Letterman's talent was 'found humour'. The writers would create a situation and drop the host in it, from which he extracted the maximum comedy completely off the cuff.

Perhaps the most successful innovation on *Late Night* has been the Top Ten List. Introduced in September 1985 it was originally planned to run just a few weeks but the idea took hold and it has been ever present since then. The idea was simple. Letterman would take a subject and read out, in reverse, ten items relating to the subject. It was perfect for one-line comments on everything ranging from current affairs and showbusiness to aspects of life in general. It also meant ten cracks at a subject so if one failed it was straight on to the next one. The idea debuted with a less than impressive 'Top Ten Things That Almost Rhyme With Peas':

10 Heats
 9 Rice
 8 Moss
 7 Ties
 6 Needs
 5 Lens

4 Ice
3 Nurse
2 Leaks
1 Meats

This ignominious beginning heralded some of the greatest writing seen on the show. The lists proved so popular that two books were published celebrating them. Letterman rates his top ten subjects and best answers as:

10 Signs that Chef Boy-Ar-Dee is Losing His Mind: *Paranoid delusion that his wife is sleeping with Uncle Ben.*
9 Pet Peeves of Indy 500 Pit Crews: *It's hard to pick up chicks while reeking of methane.*
8 Donahue Topics if Dogs Ran the Show: *Dogs who use cat doors.*
7 Things Overheard at the Moscow's McDonald's: *In ten years, when you get a car, you'll appreciate the drive-through window.*
6 Least Popular Ben & Jerry's Ice Cream Flavors: *Stuff-Found-In-Ben-&-Jerry's-Pockets.*
5 Terrifying Thoughts that Come to You as You're Falling Asleep: *Could I get a rash on the inside of my skin?*
4 Dan Quayle's National Guard Duties: *Make sure Armory's vending machines never run out of pretzel sticks.*
3 Things that will Get You Kicked Out of Disney World: *After biting into snack bar sandwich saying, 'I taste mouse'.*
2 Things Shirley MacLaine Was in Previous Lives: *Confucius groupie.*
1 John Gotti's Tax Tips: *'What H&R Block can't do, cement blocks can.'*

The standard throughout the last ten years has been superb, almost as if the writers reserved their best work for the lists. Some examples: Tricks You Can Play on the Census Taker: *Start going, '168 million and one . . . 168 million and two' so guy gets messed up and has to start counting all over again*. Amish Spring Break Activities: *Churning butter naked*. Least Popular Supermarket Chains: *Food Crypt*. Good Things About Being a Really, Really Dumb Guy: *Stallone might play you in the movie*. Least Exciting Superpowers for Comic Book Superheroes: *Ability to calm jittery squirrels*. Least Popular MTV Concerts: *With Michael Jackson's old nose*. Rejected Names for Kentucky Fried Chicken: *Hot Oily Hens*. Top Ten Signs of Spring in New York City: *Guys who usually take leaks in subway now take leaks on street*. Ways McDonalds Is Now More Health Conscious: *Ronald McDonald no longer spends night sleeping in salad bar*. Arnold Schwarzenegger's Top Ten Rejected Movie Lines: *Can you please open this jar of olives for me please*? Reasons Why It's Great to Be an American: *Attendance at Shirley MacLaine concerts not compulsory*.

> *If you're so smart how come you aren't doing something important right now?*
> Letterman to guest acknowledged as having one
> of the highest IQs in the world

The show was the antithesis of all the showbiz-bonding chat shows that had gone before. The temperature in the studio was kept at a constant chilly temperature between 48 and 52 degrees Fahrenheit, to keep both guests and audience alert. There was no warm-up man. Letterman himself appeared two minutes before taping to joke with the audience. The host wore jeans and a baseball cap and took a manic schoolboy's delight at throwing objects from windows (melons, typewriters, etc.) to witness their impact on the ground in endless slow-motion replays. His backdrop set of a window led to a running joke as he flicked index cue cards over his shoulder to the sound of breaking glass.

The whole show was an exercise in the demystification of television production, much like *That Was the Week that Was* in the 1960s. Cameras were in clear view most of the time, plus cue cards in abundance. It's not unusual for Letterman to swap with the cue-card man so he delivers the gags whilst Letterman holds up the cards. He roamed the streets once more looking for victims of his jokes and in the spirit of every good prankster made funny phone calls (Just split up with your girlfriend? Don't worry Dave will ring her on air and sort it out). In one memorable show a viewer had criticized Letterman's training shoes. A film crew and the host set out for the young girl's Long Island home to discover she wasn't home. Her brother however gladly gave a conducted tour of her bedroom and closet. Letterman then visited her at Sears department store where she worked and invited her to choose trainers for him.

A key to the show's success was the complete lack of formality with the guests. Sir Alec Guinness was interviewed after the host had thrown a carton of eggs into an electric fan. Actress Natassja Kinski was almost reduced to tears when Letterman compared her spiky hairstyle to a bonsai tree. Boxing promoter Don King of the famous electric-shock hairstyle was asked, almost upon sitting down, 'So tell me, what's the deal with your hair?' A Letterman speciality is sabotaging guests who are on to plug something. He will persistently mispronounce their name and also the film or book they are working so hard to promote. When Sharon Stone appeared to publicize her latest film the conversation was less than electrifying as she played up her sex-symbol image and as Letterman struggled to spark something interesting. When the fiasco was over Letterman turned to Paul Schaffer and announced, 'Ah, who cares.'

On one show a member of the audience was left to host the show as Letterman disappeared, 'to find my false tooth'. Book publicist Meg Parson who regularly worked late in a building opposite the studio was rung up by Letterman and crossed the street to become a guest. Since then she suffered the Three Amigos serenading her and the Jamestown High School Red Raiders marching band appearing in the street below playing Happy Birthday and spelling out M-E-G in formation. Over the years Letterman has reguarly appeared in a variety of suits covered in various objects. He has jumped into a pool wearing an Alka-Seltzer suit, dived into cheese dip wearing a Nachos suit, entered a cage of birds in a Suet Suit and been covered in milk in a Rice Krispies suit.

His anti-authority style was an immediate hit with younger viewers but it took almost two years for the show to show signs of becoming a mainstream favourite. After two years Carson held a regular nine million nightly share against Letterman's four but Letterman had the edge with advertisers; his young audience had ready-to-spend disposable income. In 1985 he told *Rolling Stone*, 'In the beginning, I thought the closer to your actual self you were on the show, the better it would be. But now I realize you definitely have to be more than yourself. You have to pretend that you're bigger than you are, that you're enjoying it more than you really are. It all has to be blown up, and you have to say and do things that you wouldn't normally have the scantest opinion on. It's just show business you know. The most pressure I'm under is when I do the *Tonight Show*. My deep fear is that Johnny won't think I'm funny.'

In 1986 the show celebrated its fourth anniversary in typical style broadcasting from a Boeing 747 en route from New York to Miami. Despite constant press raves and increasing viewing figures Letterman was almost always fatalistic that each show was a disaster and the series would soon be removed from the air. His most encouraging statements to his staff after a show might be 'Well, I guess it stuck to the videotape' or 'Nobody got killed today'. Actress Teri Garr shouted at him during a band performance on the show, 'How are you doing?' Letterman jotted down his reply on a note pad, 'I hate myself'. When Garr remonstrated with that statement he flung the pad back with the phrase underlined.

> *I'm not a talk-show host, but I play one on TV.*
> David Letterman

By 1990 Letterman was feeling the pinch from a younger contingent of late-night hosts. He had seen off a weak challenge from Joan Rivers and David Brenner in 1986 but Arsenio Hall's show began to make inroads into Letterman's viewing figures. Hall, a close friend of Eddie Murphy, brought a new black hipness to the late-night chat slot and pulled all the right levers with the audience demographics. Letterman was now aged 43 and was clearly worried that he would soon be left behind by a new and younger generation of hosts. In May 1992 he reacted badly to the news that NBC had passed him over as the natural heir to Johnny Carson and had awarded the *Tonight Show* to Jay Leno. He heard the news through press reports and it rankled that he appeared not even to have been considered. A disgruntled Letterman sounded off against the network in various interviews and made it clear he would be happy to look elsewhere when his contract was completed.

Problems had begun in 1986 when NBC were taken over by General Electric. Letterman viewed them as a monolithic organization who had no interest or passion for broadcasting. Shortly after the purchase Letterman and a camera crew went to GE headquarters with a welcoming basket of fruit for the board of directors. Letterman crossed swords with an obnoxious security man who snatched his hand away when Letterman tried to shake it. This action was mercilessly lampooned on the show as 'the GE handshake'. Plans to share the *Late Night* studio with the *Maury Povich Show* also increased the rancour. He was also unhappy with NBC for their deal with the Arts & Entertainment cable channel which gave them access to old shows. Ever one to look ahead he was displeased that in some TV markets he could be competing with his own show from almost ten years previously.

A vital element of *Late Night* is its immediacy. Taped every night between 5.30 p.m. and 6.30 p.m. it broadcasts later that night, usually in unedited form. Letterman's credo of demystifying the process of television allows only for bleeps on swearing, a network must. If there's a mistake or miscue it's rare for an edit to be introduced. As he says, 'Everything I do is designed to help me do the best job I can between 5.30 and 6.30'. He maintains the show must remain live or energy would drain out of it. It's seat of the pants stuff for the host the whole way and has kept the show fresh for the past fifteen years.

A rare exception to this rule was the appearance in October 1993 of comedian Bill Hicks (who died of pancreatic cancer in 1994). His slot on the show was cut and replaced by another comedian. Hicks made fun of bigots by pretending to be one and lambasting gays. Other material included attacks on pro-lifers and right-wing Christians. Although his act usually scored with the audience this section met with complete silence. CBS and Letterman's production company Worldwide Pants took the decision to eliminate his appearance. In a special on the star on Comedy Central after his death both David Letterman and producer Bob Morton regretted the decision made to cut out his appearance. Letterman felt anguish because Hick's death meant they could never make it up to him. This show remains unique in the *Late Night* canon as not just the most censored but also the only one where Letterman spoke the introductory voice over. Announcer Bill Wendell had gone home before the decision was made to remove Hicks.

> *It was like looking at a picture of George Washington on a dollar bill all your life and suddenly being in a bar next to him.*
> David Letterman on meeting Johnny Carson
> for the first time

Letterman had admitted many times that Carson was the only person in showbusiness he was truly in awe of. He became Letterman's idol in the 1950s when he was an avid viewer of the Carson-hosted game show *Who Do You Trust?* Since his debut on the *Tonight Show* in 1978 he had still never adjusted to being on speaking terms with his hero. When *Late Night* debuted, Carson was a co-producer and Letterman admitted, 'I'm always afraid he'll say something to me like, "Let's play tennis this weekend", I'm terrified of actually spending time with him'. In the end he did play tennis at his house but had trouble coping with the fact that Carson was on the opposite side of the net and was relieved to leave the house without breaking anything.

He expressed his fears many times in the past when the subject of the *Tonight Show* tenancy came up: 'In the back of my mind, if I weren't asked some day to do it, I'd feel kind of sad. Yet, doing it, that's my worst nightmare. That I'd be foolish enough to take the Carson position if offered to me, that I'd die a miserable death in that time slot, and meanwhile NBC had given my old show to someone who was quite happy to keep doing it. Maybe the prudent thing would be to let some other poor bastard walk into the fray for several months, and then try doing the show myself'. He later admitted however that if he had been offered the *Tonight Show* he would have taken it.

He appeared on the *Tonight Show* in August 1992 and Carson asked the obvious question about Jay Leno: 'Just how pissed off are you?' Letterman replied, 'You keep using language like that and you're going to find yourself out of a job'. Carson shot back, 'There were rumours you were going to bomb NBC.' Letterman smiled: 'I hate waiting in line.' NBC had the perfect set-up: Leno at 11.30 followed by Letterman at 12.30, two of the hottest numbers on television for a solid two hours. The crunch would come when Letterman's contract came up for renewal in 1993 but for the time being the network had it made. At this time he hired super-agent Michael Ovitz to broker a new deal for him.

> *I don't care who you are, I don't care what you do. If you have four funny stories, you can be a guest on this show. That's what we're looking for.*
>
> David Letterman

In December 1992 he was offered $14 million a year to join CBS with the understanding that his company Worldwide Pants would own and produce the show. His contract with NBC allowed them to match any offer from a rival but in the end he chose CBS. NBC were given the option to make an offer of $16 million. They played a final card by offering him the *Tonight Show* when Leno's contract ended but Letterman declined. He was off to CBS. It was rumoured at the time that if he had entered the lucrative world of syndication he could have picked up a minimum $50 million per annum and an enormous budget for the show but he wanted to stay with network television.

The news was announced on 15 January 1993. Letterman told the press, 'This will be a show for adults. Now's our chance. I didn't get to do the *Tonight Show*. This will be the show that I think I could have made the *Tonight Show*.' He told the press conference that he had spoken to Carson on the phone a few days before: 'I don't know a person in comedy or television who didn't grow up with Johnny Carson as a role model. The man has been encouraging and helpful to me in ways that he doesn't know I know about.' He was asked about Carson's advice and replied, 'He said, "Stop calling me".' NBC pre-empted the CBS announcement by organizing their own press conference affirming their belief in Jay Leno, despite their backroom manoeuvring to give Letterman his job. The cast of *Seinfeld* worked a comedy routine on the assembled press before Leno appeared on stage riding a Harley-Davidson motorbike. He brought down the house with his opening remark, 'Welcome to NBC, it means Never Believe Your Contract'.

A bitter NBC decided they owned the intellectual rights to every component of *Late Night*'s success except the host. Larry 'Bud' Melman, Stupid Pet and Human Tricks, The Top Ten List and even the name The World's Most Dangerous Band could not transfer networks, the lawyers decided. Jay Leno joked on the *Tonight Show*, 'Guests on Letterman's new show may not sit down. The idea originated with Steve Allen. Therefore, all Letterman guests must either stand or squat. Letterman may not throw a pencil through a window. Nor may he use an incendiary device to blow up a GM pick-up truck. Those are the intellectual properties of NBC. Letterman may no longer make fun of "pinhead network executives". Pinhead network executives are the exclusive property of NBC.'

As *Late Night* wound down Letterman showed as much vintage material from his eleven-year run as possible, figuring that as he was now losing control of his past he may as well utilize it as he wanted for the last time. The last show for NBC featured a Top Ten List entitled Top Ten Real Reasons I'm Leaving NBC and a stunning performance from Bruce Springsteen of 'Glory Days' after Letterman invoked him 'to blow the roof off the joint'. The proceedings ended with Letterman riding off on a white charger, in typical *Late Night* style not live, but from the eighth anniversary show.

The new show debuted on 30 August 1993, preceded by a massive media blitz. Letterman was plastered across the cover of *Time* and the *New York Times*. CBS went for broke to plug the new show as much as possible right across their primetime shows. When Letterman went to eat in Chinatown he was approached by two elderly Chinese women who asked, 'Why you go to Channel Two?' He could hardly believe that people who could barely speak English were taking an avid interest in his career. It was named the *Late Show with David Letterman* and was broadcast from the refurbished Ed Sullivan Theatre in the heart of Broadway, a project specifically undertaken for the show. Letterman had been offered the chance to move to Los Angeles but decided the uprooting of so many settled staff would prove traumatic. The Mayor of New York, David Dinkins, had gone on record as saying he would do anything to keep the show in New York including 'doing back-flips off my eyebrows'.

Larry 'Bud' Melman using his real name, Calvin DeForest, burst through the CBS eye logo, introduced Letterman and the star was off with a barbed line aimed at NBC: 'My name is Dave, and I have checked this with the CBS attorneys and legally I can continue using the name Dave.' NBC news anchor Tom Brokaw appeared and claimed two of Letterman's cue cards, announcing the jokes were the intellectual property of NBC and walked off the set. Paul Newman stood up in the audience and asked where were the singing cats. Letterman told him he was at the wrong theatre as Newman made a panicked escape up the aisle. Paul Shaffer's World's Most Dangerous Band had become The CBS Orchestra and Letterman summoned up the ghost of Ed Sullivan. Just like the first *Late Night* twelve years before, Bill Murray was the first guest. He sprayed the name Dave on Letterman's desk, advising, 'There are a lot of people who still don't know who you are.'

Letterman adopted a smarter look from day one with sharp suits and shirts. The writing matched the standard of all that had gone before in the NBC years and the 'intellectual property' problem never surfaced. The first week saw massive ratings as the effects of the massive publicity splash kicked in. Letterman had expanded his audiences with this new, universal image whilst Leno was fighting to win back younger viewers, ironically one of the reasons Carson had quit the game. As the weeks went by the *Late Show* gained and gained. It was scoring ratings that had not been seen since Carson's heyday and was reaching light-television viewers who were altering their habits to watch Letterman. This section of the audience was much prized by advertisers. Research indicated that his audience profile matched almost the regular movie-goers in the US, another fertile area for selling jeans, beer and sportswear. CBS were stunned to discover advertisers forsaking primetime fare in order to reach the younger consumer on Letterman.

One year after he went head-to-head with Leno he had beaten him in the ratings every week, even with a run of repeats against original *Tonight Shows*. But things soon began to slip. CBS (formerly known as the 'Tiffany' network as Letterman constantly reminded viewers) had made little effort to produce shows appealing to younger audiences in their primetime slots. Sitcoms and dramas based around twenty somethings were flooding the market whilst CBS soldiered on with the likes of *Murder She Wrote*. After 30 years of owning NFL football, a ratings standby, the network saw Fox outbid them to land the jewel of sports television. As Letterman commented, 'It was so discouraging to lose football. That really hurt us. To have your image associated with the NFL is so dynamic, so important.' Fox also bought New World Communications whose TV stations became Fox affiliates, dumping CBS. In major cities such as Detroit, Cleveland, Milwaukee and Atlanta, CBS was reduced to a minor player struggling to find stations willing to carry the network. In Detroit they were forced to buy a religious station, Channel 62, once known as WGPR, Where God's Power Reigns.

When Letterman signed his CBS deal he could have had little inkling of the horror story that was unfolding. 'It's so discouraging,' he said. 'In Detroit they don't even have a real building for the station. I just know we're going to be on Channel a Hundred and Seven. And I remember the days when CBS was the network everyone wanted to be with.' His employers soon became the butt of many jokes on the show. One night he held up *TV Guide* with a label attached: 'Warning: May contain CBS prime-time schedule!'

The Ed Sullivan Theatre, situated smack in the middle of Broadway, provided Letterman with a ready-made neighbourhood of real-life characters to interact with. Mujibur and Sirajul, two taciturn shop assistants from Bangladesh working at the K&L Rock America souvenir shop, became overnight stars as Letterman took the bemused pair shopping for suits or sent them coast-to-coast across America to report on what they found. Rupert Gee's delicatessen was a regular stop, with Gee sent out on to the streets with a radio receiver and asked to annoy people with inane questions supplied by Letterman, observing the action from a distance. In one classic remote Letterman took orders at a McDonald's drive-in, advising they were out of hamburgers. One customer was asked by him, 'You sound just a little depressed or something, how old are you, sir?' 'And you're pretty much happy with where you are in life?' Is it gonna be ready or what?' asked the simmering customer. Letterman replied, 'The food's ready, sure. The food will always be ready. Are you ready?'

A chance advert in a Canadian newspaper for a garage owned by Dick Assman provided an endless series of phone calls to the proprietor who became a national figure in his country. In 1994 Letterman's mother Dorothy became a star when she reported on the Montreal Winter Olympics for the show. Her down-home Midwest all-American mom image providing an alternative to the usual caustic humour. Letterman was amazed when approached by publishing houses for a deal to produce a book of his mother's recipes. To get them off his back he told his agents jokingly to ask for a million-dollar advance. This was duly paid by Pocket Books and the title went on to become a bestseller.

Letterman's private life is closely shielded. He has a large loft in New York and a major spread in New Canaan, Mass., but he rarely attends any showbiz bashes. Resolutely unmarried in his late forties, his female companions are never publicly seen with him. Letterman hit the headlines in a big way, however, in 1988 when an obsessive female fan began breaking into his home. In September of that year a woman and her young son pulled up at the tollbooth on the New Jersey side of the Lincoln Tunnel and asked if she could skip the $3 toll as she had no money. She was driving a Porsche Carrera and claimed she was Mrs David Letterman, travelling with David Letterman Jr. The police were called and a routine check revealed it was indeed Letterman's car. A call to Los Angeles, where Letterman was working, confirmed that as far as he was concerned his car was still in his garage in New Canaan. Investigating his house they found it had been broken into and the garage, of course, empty. The woman involved was named as Margaret M. Ray travelling with her son Alexander Ray, who after the arrest was placed in the care of welfare. It soon became clear that Ray had been living in the Letterman house, watering and moving plants and generally making herself at home. Letterman refused to press any charges hoping there would be no further publicity and Ray was released.

Five days later she was picked up by a cab driver outside the station in New Canaan and driven to the Letterman abode. She claimed she was his housekeeper but did not have the $7.50 fare on her. The driver witnessed her climbing in through a front window and returning with two dollars worth of change. He contacted the police and Ray was once more arrested. She had a history of mental problems and was allowed not to appear in court after psychiatric evaluation revealed she was not fit to be tried. Superior Court Judge Edward Levitt ordered her to give up trying to make any contact with Letterman in the future.

The New Canaan police department kept a close watch on the house and in February 1989 discovered Ray on the premises once more. She was found in the possession of marijuana and was charged in court with possession and trespass. The same night of her court appearance she broke into the house once more and claimed, 'I just wanted to pay him a surprise visit.' Patrolman Michael McEnaney told the press, 'She's getting to be a regular. We're on a first-name basis. Unfortunately I don't think she's a well person.' This time she was found fit to stand and given a suspended sentence. When the police had found her in the house she was wearing a watch belonging to Letterman which precipitated a further charge of larceny. Her defence regarding the watch was that she was cleaning the house and wanted to know how long it would take.

In August of 1989 she was back again when Letterman spied her moving around the grounds of the house. He discovered her raking leaves from his tennis court. The police were called once more and this time she received a nine-month prison sentence. On the news show *Current Affair* she claimed she was in love with Letterman and enjoyed writing, watching television, cleaning, washing the windows, and doing the floors. 'I like housework. I don't think there's another woman alive who could love David Letterman as much as I do. He's the dominant figure in my life.' She was released after seven months and was discovered once more in the house when Letterman returned home at 2 a.m. Finding a sink full of dirty dishes he had a shrewd idea who was in his house. When the police arrived they found Ray asleep in bed. Letterman declined to press charges, allowing her to return a week later. This time he was asleep in bed when he saw her silhouette in the doorway of the bedroom. He later claimed his reaction was, 'Oh, I know what this is. There's no trouble. I rolled over and called the New Canaan police.' She heard him on the phone and made her escape.

Things stayed quiet until July 1993 when Letterman received a note which read, 'I'm camped out on your tennis court.' The police were called and discovered she had been living there for three days and in true Margaret Ray style had been doing laundry in the swimming pool. She served a further short sentence, telling the judge, 'Mr Letterman did know I was coming. He did not respond to letters I had sent him. I think that celebrities should answer their mail.' Letterman showed great care for his nemesis. 'She is a woman who spends her days in deep confusion. She is a woman who knows few moments of lucidity or reality. She is a troubled woman who suffers great free-floating anxiety and is better when she's medicated, but not much. This woman is no more to me than a nuisance, she's not a threat.' Letterman later joked on his show that he carried a card in his wallet that said, 'In case of emergency, notify the stranger living in my house'. In August 1996 Margaret Ray made the headlines again when she was arrested for shoplifting in Carmel, Indiana, the home town of Letterman's mother Dorothy. She told the press that she had no idea that his mother lived so near.

Letterman gave his angle on talk shows in an interview with *Esquire* magazine in 1986. His theory still holds true in the nineties. 'The deal with a talk show is, it doesn't have to be stupendous. It's not great, it's not bad, it just goes by. It sticks to the videotape. It lights up the screen. Actors come on repeating the same clichés they say on every other talk show, but it doesn't matter. These things are really easy to do. They're dirt cheap. You build a set once, pay everybody as little as you can, and the guests all come on for scale. If a talk show is even moderately successful, you can nurse it along for a few years with very little expense.' He also defined lessons learnt from the past and in particular from chat-show trailblazer Jack Paar. 'You see so much happiness and so much phony effervescence and so much manufactured joy on television. In fact this is something Jack Paar told me a long time ago: 'It's okay to let people know you're upset, or pretend you're upset, because then, if they're sitting at home, they say, "Jeez, I wonder if he really is upset!"' And I've always kind of felt that there was a certain amount of truth in that.'

In 1995 Letterman hosted the Oscars for quite possibly the first and last time. His offbeat style was obviously not to the taste of most of the star-studded audience or indeed the majority of mainstream America watching. He opened by introducing Uma to Oprah and then Oprah to Keanu in a seemingly endless introductory sequence, 'Uma, Oprah, Oprah, Uma, Uma, Oprah, Keanu' etc. Tom Hanks was inveigled to help out on a Stupid Pet Trick segment and Letterman's sole film appearance in the Disney flop *Cabin Boy* was shown. His one line in the film, 'Do you wanna buy a monkey', was re-enacted by a host of celebrities on tape to a stupefied audience. The humour that was a natural to late-night audiences clearly did not cross over and Letterman was given a critical pasting. He remained unbowed, his natural dislike of the whole showbusiness façade had been played out to his biggest audience yet.

Despite the critical lambasting the Oscar ratings were the highest in twelve years. A Top Ten List the week after was headed, 'Top Ten Complaints About the Academy Awards'. The number one slot simply read 'Letterman'. Veteran director Hal Gurnee retired from the show in May 1995 with Letterman giving a valedictory to his enormous role in the host's career and his total belief in the expensive refurbishment of the Ed Sullivan Theatre to relaunch *Late Night* with CBS. A plaque was placed outside the control room in recognition of his efforts. Gurnee still acts as a consultant for the show.

In 1995 Letterman revealed some of his frustrations to *Rolling Stone* after show number 211 of his CBS run had been safely recorded. After almost fifteen years he still fretted over the way the show had gone when many in his position would have long since stopped caring. 'I wasn't very pleased with any aspect of the show. The audience and I never got together. And for me that's a lost cause.' His assessment of that show was, 'It's like a hang glider who can't get an updraft, and you're runnin' with that goddam kite on your back, and your runnin' and runnin' and there's not a breeze or a thermal or nothin'. That's what this felt like'. David Hyde Pierce from *Frazier*, comedian George Carlin and Bon Jovi had all failed to make the show click. 'Again it's my fault. I ought to be able to figure a way out to, 'Come on, we're going to fly this son of a bitch, let's go!' But I couldn't get air under the wings.'

That year had seen him deal with troublesome guests in a variety of ways. He won the Madonna bout but a smirking Mickey Rourke with a Chihuahua dog nestled in his jacket, staring into the distance all but defeated him. Nothing was happening, Rourke continued to smile inanely and Letterman tried to prise something out of him, but as he explained, 'You expect he would come out and take a punch at you and you couldn't even incite that. What I wait for now is provocation. You can't smother them. You have to kind of wait for provocation. In the old days I would smother them.' The visit of Sharon Stone was a complete non-starter. She produced a top ten list of her own on the subject of Letterman which proved a complete dud with the audience and the host but she laboured on from ten to one.

Letterman explained that after all his years in the business he still lacked the Carson touch. 'It took the wrong exit and never got back on the turnpike. Carson would have been able to harness that and turn it into something a little more low-key, a little more gracefully. I'm looking for the big KO, a knockout punch, boom, boom, stop it! The fight is stopped. It's over! Two minutes and forty seconds of the eighth round . . . Whereas Carson could just very quietly reel out a little more line, and eventually they would have sunk, and he could have handled it all by raising an eyebrow.'

One of the most telling gags currently on *Late Night* is 'Creepy Dave' where Letterman appears as a geek, through technical trickery, chatting to his svelte alter ego. In a baseball cap and jacket he often refuses to leave the set as he fires out inane observations. It's as if a hologram of Letterman in his nerdish teens has returned to haunt the big-shot chat-show host and remind him of his past. Former companion Merrill Markoe offers an image of a man always searching for success every night. 'I think that level of perfectionism is never met. It's not a wise approach to life in my opinion. It's got a sense of defeat built into it. It's like a really beautiful woman picking out flaws on her face all the time. It's the one thing that is truly important to him.'

By the end of 1995 *Late Night* began to suffer badly from CBS's prime-time plunge and was regularly being trounced by Leno on NBC and current affairs show *Nightline* on ABC. Although visibly fazed by the pressure and his Oscar-night performance Letterman still promised to deliver in the future, claiming the fall from leader gave him the chance to tell his staff, 'Boys, take the motor apart and examine each piece of it and see what's wrong.' Letterman defined the art of the chat-show host in an interview at the end of 1995. 'I'm the catalyst, I'm the reactor through which the audience interprets the show, so it's up to me to be in control and give out the right vibe. Sometimes I fail at that. Sometimes not being in synch with a guest leads to good, edgy television, and sometimes it's just, y'know, like pouring water in the toaster.'

In the autumn of 1996 the *Late Show with David Letterman* became the first late-night talk show to experiment with no commercial breaks. Advertisers would merely append their name at the beginning as in. 'This company is proud to sponsor The Late Show'. CBS executives hoped that the publicity generated would boost audiences but so far the ploy has yet to deliver results. Nevertheless, Letterman, out of all his contemporaries, is the one true originator still working today, honing his craft in a never-ending search for the perfect show.

MICHAEL ASPEL

Aspel began his broadcasting career with the BBC in 1954 as an actor on *Children's Hour* for radio. He followed on as a newsreader, then as host on *Come Dancing, Crackerjack, Give Us a Clue* and *Child's Play*. But, in his words, I'd always wanted, in a slightly masochistic way, to do a talk show. I'd been a newsreader and a disc-jockey; I'd been a reporter and a radio actor; and I'd gone round sticking microphones up the noses of people at Royal film premieres and Miss World contests until I felt I couldn't do it any longer. I'd interviewed many people on the radio and enjoyed it too, but a television talk show was something I hadn't done. Even the title came ready-made from an afternoon show that I'd done many years earlier with the BBC. It seemed to fit the bill – it got my name in, and it said what the show was about. So there was London Weekend Television, in the summer of 1983, with the idea, the title and a host who was willing and felt reasonably able.'

Aspel had already experienced a variation on the chat-show format with the BBC. The idea of that show was to dispense with any guests with any claims to fame, concentrating instead on the likes of poetry-writing dustmen. Aspel trod water in a sustained effort to keep the conversation flowing with non-professionals. The fear generated on this show obviously spread to *Aspel & Co.* when it began: 'On radio, you can go to a record or a commercial break if things get sticky. And then during those breaks, you can plan the rest of the interview, or just take a deep breath. But neither of those safety nets are available under the obelisk eye of the camera. I knew I had a lot to beat, but I also knew that I could get people to talk, and that was what made the first show a deep disappointment. I'd had years of people leaving the studio saying "I've enjoyed our talk", and I knew that I'd done a good job. So when I found myself sitting there, sweating and asking questions that I would never normally have dreamed of asking, then I thought to myself: "My boy you've lost it".'

Despite his early experiences in the format, Aspel was determined to make the lavish London Weekend show a ratings winner: 'I like talking to people and I wanted to have a stab at doing it on television. On radio, it was heartening to know that the guests who came on the show did so because they felt they'd get a good and fair hearing. I did my homework. I was keen to meet them and I enjoyed their company. So it came as a great shock to me to discover, with the first series of *Aspel & Co.*, that I'd never been so scared in my life. Here I was, 50 years old. I'd been around a while, I was used to interviewing celebrities, and to being on television. It shouldn't have frightened me, but it did.'

Aspel & Co. got underway on show one with guests Paul McCartney, Tracey Ullmann and Richard Clayderman. Audience and viewers may have been unaware of the Aspel nerves but Paul McCartney sensed the host's unease and expressed his surprise after the show that such an old trouper would be so susceptible. Aspel said, 'I've often wondered exactly what I got so scared about, although there's no denying that the show is a very exposed area. You're under attack from the word go and if you're slightly nervous, and I was more than slightly nervous, then you find that it doesn't work, and that's when the critics start honing their daggers. It does tend to sap your confidence and your vitality, particularly when you agree with the critics. You have to watch yourself afterwards, no matter how painful it is, because a series like *Aspel & Co.*

is hopefully an ongoing thing, and you've got to get it it right.'

The show played host to a stellar collection of guests that included Elizabeth Taylor, Michael Caine, Christopher Reeve, Alan Alda, Harrison Ford, Clint Eastwood and Richard Gere. It became the hottest show of its kind on television, wiping the floor with any opponents with its immense pulling power. Nevertheless, Aspel claimed, 'I enjoy the company of extrovert performers far less than people who just sit and talk. The secret of a sparkling talk lies in the combination of the guests'. Indeed Eastwood was remarkably open in his interview, lulled by Aspel's modest approach to interviews. The host could equally be tough on guests such as Joan Rivers who walked out an hour before show-time because certain demands were not met. The *Sunday Express* was full of praise: 'Anyone who can appear relaxed while presenting a chat show from what looks like the departure lounge at Luton Airport gets my attention.'

Regulars throughout the years who could always be relied on to deliver included Kenneth Williams, Roy Kinnear, Su Pollard (who did an Emu on Aspel, landing him a large lipstick laden kiss with one leg wrapped around his neck) and Jackie Collins. Mixing the standard trio of guests always brought a result, especially so with the bizarre combination of John Cleese, Julio Iglesias and Norman Tebbit. Dustin Hoffman and Sting appeared together in conversation after which Sting performed a song written by Hoffman who accompanied him on piano. The show featuring Sigourney Weaver, George Michael and Jacqueline Bissett allowed the former Wham! star to meet the woman he had always worshipped, Ms Bissett. Patrick Moore and Alan Coren joined forces with Zsa Zsa Gabor. Margaret Thatcher appeared with Barry Manilow and Tony Curtis, with Manilow convinced he could interest the prime minister in joining him at the piano to sing 'The White Cliffs Of Dover'; he failed. Mrs Thatcher revealed that, away from the world of politics and crises, at home she 'just liked to potter around the house, turn out a few drawers' and accidentally confessed, 'I'm always on the job'. The interview with Curtis was severely truncated by the star who objected to Aspel's opening remark, 'What is it like to be the last of the old-style studio creations?' Midway through the interview, Curtis had had enough, stood up, said, 'I bid you good night' and disappeared.

On technique, Aspel reveals, 'I just try to make sure I look at the person I'm talking to, and show them I'm interested. You've got to be interested. I'd rather not talk to the guests much before-hand simply because I find it works better just to say hello, and thanks for coming, and leave it at that. The last thing you want is to start an involved conversation because when you come to do it for real it can all seem a bit stale.' Sir Robin Day lost his temper on the show with another guest, Ben Elton, whom he told, 'I'd just love to get your jowls and slap them together. Can I do that to you.' The incident happened after Elton interrupted Day in full flow by passing a comment on Sir Winston Churchill and being asked by Day, 'Would you shut up for two minutes?' After a second interjection from Elton, Day let fly with, 'I said shut up.' Elton inquired, 'Sir Robin are you really going to sit here and have a go?' On telling Day he was 'prickly tonight', Day shot back with, 'You haven't stopped talking for the last half hour.' The programme, however, unfortunately went down the same road as *Wogan* with a Planet Hollywood special starring Arnold Schwarzenegger, Bruce Willis and Sylvester Stallone. With a great touch of irony Aspel recognised the brazen advertising involved and at one point began to read from the menu. They went one step worse than *Wogan* too by showing commercials for the restaurant.

Of the taxing effects of interviewing, Aspel remembers: 'Much later when the show and I were in our stride, Wayne Sleep was a guest and he talked about the pain of being a dancer. He said, "At least Sebastian Coe can look absolutely exhausted as he runs to the tape. I always think of dancing as being like running the hundred yards with a smile on your face!" And I think that just about sums up how I felt during those first shows.' Richard Gere was unhappy to say the least when Aspel introduced him as a sex symbol. 'The whole thing about a talk show is that you have to ask the questions that people are interested in, not in a way that puts the guest on the spot or makes them feel awkward, we're not out to get anyone, that's not the idea at all, but certain things must be asked. If the guest doesn't want to answer, that's up to him or her but Richard Gere took exception to the introduction I gave him and when it came to the commercial break, he waggled his finger at me.'

When Chuck Berry was asked by Aspel what song he would be performing he replied, 'Small fee, small hit!' True to style Berry refused to leave his hotel to record the show unless London Weekend delivered his fee beforehand in cash. The interview with a Hollywood actress packed plenty of hard-hitting punches. The actress was shown the famous photo of herself when she had ballooned to over 200 pounds in weight. 'I have to ask,' said Michael, 'where does all the skin go. Has it involved plastic surgery?' Hardly the questions of a soft-pedalling interviewer.

Many US guests asked to see a tape of the show before agreeing to book an appearance and many felt the host was somewhat forward. Researchers soon gave up trying to attract big US names by telephone but opted to travel to their homes for preliminary discussions and give them some idea of what they could expect. The researchers (mainly female and known as Aspel's Angels) would then produce a biography which in some cases could extend beyond 40 pages. Details were listed of celebrity quirks. Julio Iglesias only films from the right for example. Aspel would then study his future guest's appearances on US chat shows, this extra material providing a safety net if things got rocky. 'The thing about talk shows is that you just never know how they'll turn out. It all depends on the mood of the guest, the combination of people we have on, and a million other unforseeable factors. A good guest, one who'll really deliver the goods, has to play the game. It means knowing what the show requires and not what their ego needs.'

Some idea of Aspel's modesty can be seen in the fact that at the age of 40, in 1973, with close on twenty years of showbiz experience, he fulfilled his childhood dream of visiting the US. 'When the pilot said that the lights of Boston were visible below I dropped everything and rushed to the other side of the aircraft to look. The feeling I got from seeing them was colossal. I remember thinking, it didn't matter what happened to me afterwards, whether the plane crashed or we had to turn back. I'd seen America.'

On the famed 1987 show with a drunken Oliver Reed staggering around with a pitcher of orange juice (containing an unnamed spirit) Aspel asked, 'I've read that you once drank 104 pints in 24 hours. Is it true?' Reed replied, 'No, it was 48 hours.' Aspel's sanguine reply was, 'Oh that's all right then.' After Reed performed a ramshackle version of Billy Idol's 'Wild One' with the house orchestra he accused fellow guest Clive James of being drunk. James later admitted, 'It was one of the most exciting evenings I've had since World War II when I was much further from the front.'

The defining moment of Aspel's complete lack of guile occurred during a show featuring Jackie Collins and Pamela Stephenson. Asked what his pet name for his penis was, he shot back instantly that he called it his dickie without a trace of embarrassment. When asked by Jackie Collins at what age he had lost his virginity (a difficult enough question for any man, let alone in front of ten million viewers), after Aspel had raised an eyebrow over a scene in one of her books where a thirteen-year-old girl had lost hers, he gave her an instant answer with no trace of bashfulness; 'I was a virgin soldier. I came out of National Service a virgin. I was 37, no, 20.' Aspel was quite happy to let a guest plug on the programme as long as they talked about something else during the interview. His near anonymity saw him blend into the background backstage: 'There's always an entourage of partners, agents, drivers, bodyguards and so on. But most of them don't know who I am so I just say excuse me and slip past.'

He quit the whole format in 1993 'because it wasn't fun anymore. Many stars are scared witless talking about themselves, they won't play the game.' The excitement of having Warren Beatty on the show summed it all up for him. The legendary film star had absolutely nothing to say, much like Paul Newman who provided sparkling conversation before and after but not during the show. Despite a contract worth over half a million he could no longer be second fiddle to Hollywood stars. 'It's part of the trick to look as though you're enjoying it, but I wasn't. You have to be more and more ingratiating and I just got tired of that sitting at their feet and going through the motions. I don't think the chat show has had its day, but the idea of good intelligent conversation is becoming harder to find, the more private people are staying away.' From a ten million high the Aspel audience had sunk to below five million. *Aspel & Co.* perhaps summed up the false glamour of the eighties but there is no doubt that it left a large vacuum when it departed and nothing of its calibre has replaced it.

OPRAH WINFREY

On TV, Oprah's gift is her interest in so many things and she asks the questions people really want to know. She has no inhibitions. She doesn't worry about her image or her credibility. She just asks from her gut.

Maria Shriver

The American Dream, to rise out of poverty to wealth and success, has been achieved by many. Few, however, can match the ascent of Oprah Winfrey from being born illegitimate, living on a Mississippi pig farm and then becoming the richest entertainer in America (and thus the world). At her present state of earning Winfrey is on course to become a billionaire by the year 2000. She is the most famous woman in America. If she puts on weight (or even takes it off) the nation soon knows, either through her talk show or through the tabloid press. She is comparable to the Princess of Wales in terms of media coverage, her love life, her friends and her finances are all under the most public of scrutiny.

Her rise to showbiz fame was relatively short and the *Oprah Winfrey Show* has now become the talk show that all others are measured by. She was by no means the first in her field: Phil Donahue had originated the audience participation and controversial subject idea in the 1960s but with Winfrey the idea took wing. The main factor was her directness. She asked the questions the audience would have, and required an answer from even the biggest celebrity. When dealing with emotional topics she often cried and hugged participants, giving her immediate empathy with viewers. It was no showbiz cliché. Oprah Winfrey really cares and proves it with her constant campaigning for various causes. In the facile world of US television Oprah Winfrey stands head and shoulders above the rest as someone who really does give a damn.

Born on 29 January 1954 in Kosciusko, Mississippi and named after Orpah from the Old Testament's Book of Ruth, her name was misspelt by a midwife or registrar. Abandoned by her mother Vernita she was brought up by her grandmother Hatti Mae. She spent the first six years of her life barefoot in a pig-farm house with no running water, sanitation or television. With few friends and no toys the infant Winfrey was raised on a diet of religion and discipline. It's hard to reconcile these images of poverty in the America of the 1950s when consumerism began to take hold of the country and millions enjoyed a new prosperity. In 1960 her mother reappeared and took her daughter to live in Milwaukee. This proved short-lived and she was passed on to her father Vernon and his wife Zelma. Here began a strict regime of study from her stepmother where she had to read a book a week and report on it. She moved back with her mother and entered a long period of delinquency.

Unpopular at school, it is claimed she was sexually abused by a relative. This led to a long period of sexual trauma. By the age of thirteen she had become a teenage tearaway, running completely out of control. When Oprah discovered that she was pregnant, she returned to the family home for support. Sadly her baby was born prematurely and died soon after birth. By now her life had started to take a different direction. Moving to Nashville she was subjected to a new disciplinarian lifestyle by her father with an emphasis on education and prim, ladylike behaviour. Few of her friends from Milwaukee would have recognised the new self-confident girl determined to study and do well in her life. With such a turbulent early life it's perhaps understandable how Winfrey finds it easy to interact with her guests and audience.

She gained her first experience of broadcasting on Nashville radio station WVOL. Still at high school she had called at the station to pick up a watch, a prize for winning a Miss Fire Prevention contest. One of the disc-jockeys was impressed by her resonant voice and she was taken on as a part-timer, learning all the basics of broadcasting. She entered the all-black Tennessee State University and in March 1972 won Miss Black Nashville and Miss Black Tennessee, later becoming a runner up in Miss Black America. Shortly after she was offered a job in television by Nashville station WTVF-TV. She quit college and became Nashville's first-ever black newscaster. Under no illusions, Winfrey has since admitted, 'No way did I deserve the job. I was a classic token.' But it gave her a three-year grounding in the mechanics of television.

In the summer of 1976, aged 22, she moved on to Baltimore and the next stage of her career. Joining WJZ-TV she was taken on to act as co-anchor for an expanded hour-long local news show. The Federal Communications Commission were keen to promote desegregation in television and with Baltimore's large African–American population, a black co-anchor made sense. However, for a period her name was changed bizarrely to Cindy Winfrey and she was promoted as coming from an Hispanic background. A New York hair salon ruined her hair in an attempt to make her look Puerto Rican and she was left almost bald. Reduced to wearing ill-fitting wigs, the once lithe young woman binged on food – what would become an habitual reaction to problems in her life.

It was during these news bulletins that the Oprah Winfrey style began to develop. She found it impossible to be dispassionate when reporting on the stories of death and murder in the city. When she interviewed a mother who had lost seven children in a fire she apologized to viewers that her grief had shown through.

In the spring of 1977 she was switched to a morning talk show called *People Are Talking* co-hosted with Richard Sheer. Broadcast against the *Phil Donahue Show*, then the highest-rated daytime talk show, many of the backroom staff thought the show was doomed to failure. Producer Sherry Burns saw Winfrey's appeal instantly: 'She's the universal woman. She gets right past the black thing. She's a totally approachable, real, warm person.'

Mainly unscripted, the show flowed entirely on the whims of Winfrey's questions as she delved through her guests, probing deftly and revealingly. Soon the show was outperforming *Donahue* in the Baltimore area and was repeated at night. Controversial topics were introduced ranging from adultery to incest and ratings continued to soar. In 1983 producer Debra DiMaio quit the show and joined WLS-TV in Chicago to produce *A.M. Chicago*. Winfrey soon followed her and in January 1984 made her debut in one of America's largest cities and TV markets. Within a week her ratings equalled that of *Donahue* and within three months were ahead of him.

> *She's Oprah Winfrey, zaftig gab queen, soaking up the bubble bathos of life and threatening to send poor, yakked out Phil Donahue into video menopause.*
>
> *Washington Post*

In Chicago she entered the fast lane of television, interviewing stars like Paul McCartney, Tom Selleck and Goldie Hawn and was an instant success. By the end of 1984 she was the number one TV personality in Chicago. In his book *Oprah Winfrey – The Real Story*, George Mair defined the difference between Winfrey and other talk-show hosts: 'When Donahue interviews a hooker who services twenty men a night, he wants to know how much money she makes. Oprah wants to know if she's sore. When Donahue interviews Dudley Moore, he asks about his next movie. Oprah wants to know how such a short man can make love to all the very tall girlfriends Moore has had. When

Donahue interviews a satanist, he wants to know where devil worshippers go when they die. Oprah wants to know if her guest has personally made human sacrifices of small children on the altar of Satan. It was Oprah who asked Sally Field if Burt Reynolds wore his toupée while they made love and Michael Jackson if he was still a virgin. Who else would have the nerve but Oprah?'

Guests on the show have admitted that Winfrey had the ability to get them to answer any question. She explains the show's success thus: 'We go for the gut. We go for the absolute gut. My theory is that everybody is the same. I want the same thing that people in Spokane want: to be loved. So we try to pick subjects that everybody can relate to, and do it in such a way that every single person who's watching can listen to us and say, "Yeah, that's it. I know exactly what you're talking about".' In January 1985 Phil Donahue admitted defeat and pulled out of Chicago and re-located to New York after being caned in the ratings by Winfrey.

She amazed everyone during a programme on child abuse by revealing her own suffering and winning the hearts of viewers everywhere. If her shoes hurt she would take them off on the show, she told the audience how much she hated her broad nose and she confided her most intimate eating secrets with them. On one show she revealed that on one evening her freezer was bare so she snacked on hot-dog buns covered in maple syrup. Scripts went out the window, her production team fed her background material and she asked questions as they occurred to her. Her control became total: within the year she decided who the guests on the show would be and what topics would be under discussion.

Chicago magazine declared, 'The Oprah Winfrey Show has been one of the true astonishments of television. Single-handedly, she and it have revolutionized talk shows and rendered the notion of Midwestern reticence quaint and obsolete. No one else on television has been as open as Oprah. Within months of coming to Chicago she'd told viewers about her troubles with men, her weight problems and the terrifying history of her childhood sexual abuse. She told them they could take control of their life energies and gave them the practical means of doing so.' In January of 1985 the first glimmer of national recognition called when Winfrey was a guest on the *Tonight Show*. From then on the rise to fame was mercurial. She found a national audience once more with her Oscar-nominated role in Steven Spielberg's film *The Color Purple*. *A.M. Chicago* had changed to the *Oprah Winfrey Show* and most importantly, with her new-found star power, she decided to syndicate the show to a national audience.

King World Productions, syndicators of the massively successful *Wheel of Fortune* and *Jeopardy*, made a deal with the newly formed Harpo Productions and sold the show to 180 TV stations across America. The first week of shows featured how to catch a man, fighting families, a baby refused a heart transplant because his parents weren't married, neo-Nazis and women raped by their doctors. The programme became an instant hit, with Winfrey telling reporters, 'It's going to do well. If it doesn't, I will still do well. I will do well because I am not defined by a show. I think we are defined by the way we treat ourselves and the way we treat other people.' In 1986, its first year in syndication, the show earned $125 million, its star receiving a $30 million salary. The lucrative world of TV talk shows is underlined by the fact that the *Oprah Winfrey Show* currently costs approximately $200,000 a week to produce but grosses close to $20 million a week in syndication fees. By the old adage, it really is a licence to print money.

Any book that appeared on the show became a runaway success, underlining Winfrey's massive influence on America's daytime female audience. Robert James Waller's romantic novel *The Bridges of Madison County* was featured on the show in a broadcast from one of the bridges and went on to become one of the biggest-selling books in publishing history. Callan Pinckney's exercise book and video *Callanetics* was a non-starter on publication but soared to bestselling heights after a feature on the show. In the late eighties, the early days of the video retail market, the video became Britain's bestseller. In 1988 Winfrey became owner of her show and built her own studio in Chicago, the first black to own a major studio in the US. During this period she produced and starred in the TV movie *The Women of Brewster Place*, about seven women living in a run-down apartment block, which later inspired a full series. In one of her first tastes of failure it was cancelled after just four episodes, many critics dubbing it a black version of *The Waltons*.

By the late eighties America could not get enough of Oprah Winfrey with two subjects dominating tabloid headlines. Her weight was a major issue and a gain or loss on the scales became front-page news. Not since singer Kate Smith or Elizabeth Taylor had America been so interested by a celebrity's weight. Her show on 15 November 1988 titled Diet Dreams Come True was a landmark in US daytime television with 45% of viewers watching it. After resorting to a liquid diet she lost 67 pounds and proudly advertised the fact by appearing on the show tugging a trolley containing that amount in animal fat. Most women worldwide are weight-conscious and in this one show Winfrey struck a chord: despite being a major TV personality, her problems were akin to those of her audience. Her personal chef Rosie Daley, an expert at cooking with fat-free ingredients saw sales of her book *In the Kitchen with Rosie* soar when she appeared on the show.

The other major interest was her long-standing relationship with Stedman Graham Jr. Their romance has kept America waiting with bated breath over the years for a marriage announcement. Exchanging expensive gifts and taking exotic holidays has kept the US press-pack employed for years. The *National Enquirer* reguarly prints fuzzy photos of the couple enjoying themselves on luxury yachts in dream locations and asking the question, when? In a TV interview she claimed she was asked the question over ten times a day.

I don't know anything about oil or gold. I've been doing television since I was nineteen, and TV is what I know and understand.

Oprah Winfrey

At the beginning of the nineties *Time* magazine declared, 'Few would have bet on Oprah Winfrey's swift rise to host of the most popular talk show on TV. In a field dominated by white males, she is a black woman of ample bulk. As interviewers go, she is no match for, say, Phil Donahue. What she lacks in journalistic toughness, however, she makes up in plainspoken curiosity, robust humour and, above all, empathy. Guests with sad stories to tell are apt to rouse a tear in Oprah's eye. They, in turn, often find themselves revealing things they would not imagine telling anyone, much less a national TV audience. It is the talk show as group-therapy session.' The opposition was now hotting up with a dawn-to-dusk array of talk shows filling the screens but Winfrey still held her position as market leader.

The American public is becoming the most over-informed uninformed people on earth, a nation of boob-tube boobs spoon-fed nothing but low-fiber fluff.

Tom Shales

After the rapid growth of shock daytime talk shows with controversial subjects a backlash began. Talk-show host Geraldo Rivera seethed, 'I'm sick of trash TV! Shows like Oprah and Donahue and even my own have gone over the line and we've all got to stop piping sleazy, perverted material into America's homes! I'm the first to say, "I'm stopping it!" Now it's time for the others to follow. Oprah, enough of the sleaze! Daytime talk shows have covered such shocking topics as sex with animals, sex-change operations, lesbian marriages, incest, and worse. And it seems that with each passing week, the topics get more and more bizarre.' Tom Shales of the *Washington Post* railed against Winfrey and her contemporaries: 'The daily parade: wackos, loonies, stars, celebrities, freaks, geeks and gurus. Much of it is appallingly entertaining, little of it is remotely worthwhile. On one of her few serious, outer-directed shows, Winfrey dealt with declining literacy among the young and the escalating crisis in American education. In promos she looked into the camera and asked, "How dumb are we?" There's every possibility that talk rot is making us dumber.'

The line with the *Oprah Winfrey Show* is to ignore all criticism as the entire production deems itself head and shoulders above all daytime talk shows. Oprah herself did reply to her detractors: I'm really proud of the *Oprah Winfrey Show*. Every day my intention is to empower people, and my intention is for other people to recognize by watching our show that you really are responsible for your life. I think I can be a catalyst for people beginning to think more insightfully about themselves and their lives.

The year 1991 saw the launch of a crusade to protect children from abuse. Horrified by the death of four-year-old Angelica Mena of Chicago, who was raped, murdered and thrown into a lake by a next-door neighbour, she began a series of shows on the suffering of children in America. The National Child Protection Bill, or as it became known, Oprah's Bill, was put before the Senate to create a national registry of child abusers with Winfrey giving testimony. In 1994 the bill was made law with Winfrey standing at President Clinton's side as he signed it into law at the White House. A programme on child abuse, *Scared Silent: Exposing and Ending Child Abuse* created broadcast history when it was shown on NBC, CBS, ABC and PBS. Narrated by Winfrey it opened with the statement, 'I'm Oprah Winfrey, and like millions of other Americans, I'm a survivor of child abuse. I was only nine years old when I was raped by my nineteen-year-old cousin. He was the first of three family members to sexually molest me.'

Another programme that sent ratings soaring was the February 1992 telecast: an interview with Michael Jackson at his Neverland ranch. The show was seen in 39.3% of all US homes and had a 56% share of all sets turned on at transmission time. It was Jackson's first interview in fourteen years. No question was spared as Jackson was subjected to an interview blitz on his virginity, family and skin tone. *Jet* magazine reported that 'Oprah' had entered many American teenager's vocabulary as a word meaning 'to engage in persistent, intimate questioning with the intention of obtaining a confession; usually used by men of women, as in, "I wasn't going to tell her, but after a few drinks, she oprah'd it out of me".'

In 1993 she made the cover of *Forbes* magazine as the richest entertainer in America and thus the world. Her earnings showed that the *Oprah Winfrey Show* was seen in over 99% of US TV markets and in 64 countries. Her slice of the income had amounted to $46 million in 1992 and $52 million in 1993. In the autumn of 1996 *Forbes* confirmed Winfrey was once more the highest-paid entertainer in the world. She received an estimated £114 million in the previous two years. Steven Spielberg was second with £100 million followed by the Beatles at £83 million. Winfrey amazed American audiences once more in 1995 when she admitted on the show she had smoked cocaine during her years in Baltimore in the 1970s. As the talk-show war begins to cool down with pretenders falling by the wayside as each set of ratings are published Oprah Winfrey looks set to outlast them all.

TERRY WOGAN

It is said that I am bigger than the people I interview. That of course is the essence of the show. In terms of popularity, notoriety or fame – whatever you call it – I'm as big if not bigger than the people I'm interviewing. That's why people watch.

Terry Wogan

Terry Wogan entered broadcasting in November 1961 when he relinquished a secure job in a bank in Dublin, where he had worked for five years, to join state broadcaster Radio Eireann. Under the title of 'radio announcer' he linked programmes, read the news and set the scene at the beginning of plays. He progressed to hosting such daytime staples as *Hospital Requests* and *Rogha Na Mban* – literally 'Lady's Choice', Ireland's version of the BBC's *Housewives Choice*. He soon progressed to television newsreader with RTE and then found fame when he replaced Gay Byrne (long-time host of Irish chat feast *The Late Late Show*) on the quiz *Jackpot*.

The top quiz on television, its formality was soon replaced by Wogan's humour, constant ad-libbing and complete send-up of the whole genre. His new approach and good looks won over many viewers but alienated others. Fellow broadcaster Maurice O'Doherty claimed, 'I felt that the plain people of Ireland did not care a lot for Terry as a presenter; Gay Byrne was more their man. It was the early days of television and Terry's impish sense of humour was inclined to alienate members of the public who interpreted his mockery as somewhat hurtful. Ironic Limerick humour was not well known to people from other areas of the country, and they just didn't like it.'

Wogan saw it another way: 'One way of doing a show like *Jackpot* is to give oneself a smooth synthetic gloss, like a Hughie Green, able to cope with any situation. Another way, my way, is try to be human and natural and sincere. I can't do the quick-fire stuff. I'm introspective, I suppose maybe it's the boy philosopher coming out in me. It's impossible to be truly yourself. If you concentrate on being yourself you're just not. Experience gives me confidence, nothing else really.' Taking over a national institution like *Jackpot* after the insular world of radio proved a shock: 'It was a nightmare experience. I just couldn't cope with the technology. I had come from the more intimate medium of radio, where there was only me in the studio and a producer and two soundmen working with me, to this huge television studio with what seemed hundreds of technicians and those enormous cameras looking at me.' When the BBC relaunched their radio network in 1967 with Radios 1, 2, 3 and 4, Wogan, in common with other Irish broadcasters, sent a demo tape of his work, desperate to broaden his horizons. It landed on the desk of Mark White, the man assigned to find new talent for the all-new pop station Radio 1. Dave Lee Travis, Tony Blackburn, Emperor Rosko and Kenny Everett had all been signed by him for the fledgeling station. The demo tape did not initially impress however: an anxious Wogan had posted it wound back to front. White liked what he heard straight away: 'Here was a bright, cheerful and absolutely natural sounding voice. There was no trace of pretension. It sounded as if he liked the music he was playing, and talking to people. It was the complete opposite to many tapes we were receiving.'

Wogan was offered a contract and, like Eamonn Andrews

twenty years before him, made the decision to commute from his Irish home to build the foundations of a career in London. He appears in the classic photograph taken on the steps of All Souls, opposite Broadcasting House, amongst the original Radio 1 roster. At the peak of the Summer of Love and the flower people he doesn't look out of place in his smartly conservative suit, white shirt and tie. Jimmy Young smiles benignly behind him, with Bob Holness to his right, and apart from John Peel everyone is similarly besuited and eager to please. This was the BBC's answer to pirate radio.

Wogan is described in Keith Skues' book *Radio Onederland* as 'one of the best known names on radio and television in Ireland. On Radio Eirean his scope is wide, as a disc-jockey, compere, newsreader, announcer, interviewer and as a presenter of documentary programmes'. He made his debut on the quaintly titled *Midday Spin* and then graduated shortly after to *Late Night Extra*, a simultaneous broadcast on Radios 1 and 2. With an increasing workload in both Dublin and London he made the decision to become a freelancer. With his Irish bosses becoming more intolerant of his new-found English success Wogan decided to make the break from presenting such programmes as *Terry Awhile* and *Children's Forum* to join the BBC full time.

His big radio break came in 1969 when he filled in for Jimmy Young on his afternoon show, another programme simultaneously broadcast on Radios 1 and 2. His languid wit and style became an instant hit with listeners. At the age of 31 he became the afternoon mainstay for Radio 1. The *Fight the Flab* spot became a national institution with listeners and irate company owners were regularly featured in newspapers complaining that female staff stopped work immediately to follow the Wogan exercise instructions. He joined the elite club alongside Tony (Arnold!) Blackburn and Jimmy (What's the recipe today Jim?) Young as the only DJs with long-term contracts at the BBC. He assessed his appeal: 'I've a classless accent, in England they judge you by your accent, but the Irish can't be categorised. I say things a bit differently. I don't write scripts. It's all spontaneous. Sometimes it works, sometimes it doesn't.

Most of the time it did work as the Reveille DJ of the Year award proved. Third behind Tony Blackburn and Jimmy Savile in the 1969 ratings he moved up to number two in 1970 behind Tony Blackburn. In 1972 his mentor Mark White was given the task of re-aligning Radio 2 and immediately negotiated for him to take over the *Breakfast Show*. Audiences soared to eight million as Wogan got into his stride with his whimsical musings on the view from the studio across the rooftops of London. He created pictures across the airwaves of the BBC director general shaving at a window, bringing in his milk, cows grazing and BBC staff frolicking in the Broadcasting House open-air swimming pool. He touched a chord with Middle England, unheard before on British radio and became part of the rich tapestry of the BBC alongside *The Archers* and *Desert Island Discs*. As well as *Fight The Flab*, *Wogan's Winners*, which gave hot racing tips, became part of the national psyche. The Queen was known to be a keen listener and the Queen Mother once had a request played.

The highlight of many listener's day was the 10 a.m. handover to Jimmy Young when the two regaled listeners with light-hearted insults and genial banter. 'I had time on the *Breakfast Show* to develop my sense of humour. There was no comparable show on Irish radio so there was no scope for this kind of development. I could talk as I liked. I was doing what I liked doing. Spontaneity was and is my forte. It's as simple as that. I don't mean to say that everybody liked my breakfast show. I'm sure many didn't; there's always been a love-hate thing between me and my listeners and viewers. In Irish radio we were bedevilled by old-fashioned practices. RTE didn't trust their broadcasters to ad lib. I was always encouraged by the BBC to ad-lib, to be spontaneous. The BBC give you credit for intelligence and maturity. They give you the microphone and you're in control. You were in charge of what you were doing. I put no limit on my ad-libbing, for instance. I let it flow.'

The Bionic Man is already with us, not just in fictional but factual form. What else is Terry Wogan, for example, but a Six Million Dollar Man with a shamrock in his buttonhole.

Clive James

Wogan made early inroads on to television with beauty competitions, *Come Dancing*, *Disco*, *Startown*, *What's on Wogan*, *Lunchtime with Wogan* and *They Sold a Million* but made his mark when, in 1978, the BBC decided to adopt the US game show *Blankety Blank* for British audiences with him as host. A simple enough concept – celebrities filled in missing words for contestants to guess – he turned the whole idea on its head. As director Marcus Plantin relates, 'Terry enjoyed the duels with the stars on the panel; the rapport between them was scintillating. Since the show wasn't scripted it gave him scope to ad-lib. Spontaneity has always been his forte, so *Blankety Blank* was up his street. Terry made a laugh of the crummy prizes, mocked them, but this became part of the fun. Terry is brilliant at the art of depreciation. In a funny way, he broke all the rules, with the result that *Blankety Blank* was really a parody on the game show itself. Doing it helped his television career.'

The irreverence, always witty and never cynical, honed on almost twenty years of radio broadcasting, blossomed as he roamed the *Blankety Blank* stage, never hidebound behind a desk. The BBC Annual Report for 1979 pompously described the show as, 'harmless fun handled skillfully by Terry Wogan yet the prominence of its success in the schedules led to the suggestion that the whole network has become trivialised'. During this period he became synonymous with the Eurovision Song Contest as host and jocular commentator, a role he still fulfils to this day. He reached the heights of British showbusiness in November 1982 with a Variety Club dinner held in his honour.

With all his conversational skills the role of chat show seemed a natural progression but his first attempt in the medium was not a success. A Saturday-night show launched in May 1982 was a ratings hit, with the host christened 'Baron of the Blarney', but he was disappointed that it was recorded and only a once-a-week vehicle. The first show kicked off with audience pleaser Bruce Forsyth and followed with a further two series, the latter up against the *Jimmy Young Television Show* on ITV. Wogan made it clear to the critics, 'I am not the new Parkinson, I am the old Wogan.' He attempted on this series to prevent US stars using the show to do their act or plug books and films. 'British artists are no problem but Americans are used to the Johnny Carson method. People like Joan Rivers and Victoria Principal expect to be told the questions they are going to be asked in advance. I refuse point blank.'

This late-night slot acted as a valuable primer for the future. After having Michael Parkinson as a guest he felt he had finally defined the Wogan interviewing style. 'I've tried to be more humorous, more spontaneous. I don't want a confrontation with my guests. I don't want to be controversial or come on like Sir Robin Day.' During this period he held down his Radio 2 job but in October 1984 it was announced he was quitting radio to host a thrice weekly live chat show for the BBC early in the new year.

> *Terry is the BBC's greatest asset.*
>
> Michael Grade

David Frost had been the first person to attempt to follow the US chat-show style in Britain, with his band of Friday-to-Sunday programmes for LWT but no one had attempted to use the *Tonight Show* formula right across weekday nights. The Frost shows included audience participation and debated serious topics alongside standard showbiz fare. Wogan was slotted into the schedule at 7 p.m. on Monday, Wednesday and Friday nights with an intent to keep the audience with BBC1 from early evening onwards. The aim was a lightweight, relaxed formula with a cross-section of stars, authors, musicians and people in the news. Politics and current affairs were studiously avoided. Wogan laid down his rules from the beginning. 'I am different. Parkinson interviews. What I want is conversation. He is a journalist by training. I've no journalistic training. I shall act more as a catalyst and not give my guests a hard ride. I'd like to get them away from their routine, which they've done for everyone else.'

The BBC were keen to kick off with a major-league guest and Mick Jagger was approached, but after lengthy negotiations the Rolling Stones front-man turned it down. Elton John, Tina Turner, Wendy Richard and Rory Bremner were the guests for the opening show on 18 February 1985. Despite claims that the show was not about celebrities plugging books, films or TV shows the opener consisted mainly of just that. Wendy Richard was there to promote the new BBC soap *EastEnders*, scheduled to make its bow the next evening. A further attention grabber appeared in the shape of Tory councillor Christine Smith from Sheffield who had presented the prime minister with a petition consisting of 3,000 signatures from angry *Dallas* fans, upset that the Corporation had allowed themselves to be outbid by Thames to retain rights to the new series. Wogan jokingly deflected her anger and then made the first public announcement that the BBC had now repurchased the show and it would air in March. However Wogan made the news headlines the next day not because of a pitched argument or controversy but simply because he fell over when greeting guest Elton John. It set the tone for the series. The *Daily Express* raved over show one, 'Unquestionably it was the most spectacular launch of any new show I can ever remember.'

Ironically Wogan's fellow countryman Eamonn Andrews became his nemesis as the all-out battle between the BBC and ITV for the early-evening viewing share escalated. ITV used Eamonn Andrews in a revival of his panel game *What's My Line* to deflate the Monday-night *Wogan* show and by March the fledgeling talk show had failed to crack the top ten viewing figures. Much was made of the fact that *Parkinson* had reguarly attracted fifteen to twenty million viewers in a late-night Saturday slot against early-evening *Wogan* with just ten million. ITV hit back further by scheduling their new medical soap *The Practice* up against the Friday *Wogan*.

The first major guest was Princess Anne, on a show recorded in advance for security reasons. A child in Glasgow had asked Princess Anne on a visit why she had never appeared on *Wogan*. She was told that she had never been asked, spurring the production team into action. This show alone attracted thirteen million viewers and was to prove the most successful in the early days. ITV used their Eamonn Andrews' joker once more when in May *This Is Your Life* was placed up against *Wogan*. The most simplistic happenings on the show became running gags. When Sophia Loren told the host that her book on beauty laid special emphasis on the legs he invited her to touch his, a request she declined. After that a standard entrée for guests was a ritual 'laying of hands' on the legs.

The press began to clamour for a more rigid style of interviewing instead of the exchange of pleasantries and plugging. By year end much was being made about the low-brow content of the show. Alasdair Milne, the BBC director general, told *Broadcast* magazine, 'Wogan's so good on his feet and so experienced now I think we can take the show up a notch.' Wogan replied, 'I have my bow-tie and horn-rimmed glasses at the ready.' The year finished on a low point with the much-maligned *Wogan* Christmas special from the *Dynasty* set, Carrington mansion. The glamorous actors and actresses from the tacky US soap engaged in vacuous chat of stunning banality capped by Blake's message, 'Good wishes to the wonderful people over there in Britainland'. Whilst in the US for the show Wogan appeared as a guest on the *Merv Griffin Show*, introduced to the audience as Britain's premier chat-show host, to complete apathy. 'I must say I was impressed with Merv. He owns the theatre, owns the show and sells the programmes to the networks. I decided to have a long talk with the BBC when I got back.' He also became determined to make *Wogan* a five-nights-a-week show in the US style.

As the programme celebrated its 200th show the master of TV inquisition Sir Robin Day gave vent to his feelings. 'I don't know why it has become popular. It began in the BBC as something of an illegitimate baby. It appeals to academics, professors and politicians. I could never be over-exposed like Terry Wogan. After all I'm on thirty weeks a year and then only once a week.' Surprisingly Sir Robin had been a guest on the Saturday-night show and had told Wogan he was better at his job than Michael Parkinson. His leg had been touched on that show and Day had claimed he would make a citizen's arrest. Day had been appalled by the *Dynasty* show claiming it was, 'even more boring than I am'. Sir Robin appeared on *Wogan* shortly after (cunningly wearing a tie in preference to a dickie-bow) and defended his stance against the host who although smiling, dealt with him in an uncompromising fashion.

As ratings began to fall off for the show the critics were prepared to pounce. Wogan's £350,000-a-year salary was high-lighted in most press interviews. His answer? 'They say I earn this kind of money. I don't think that's much per programme. It makes me the lowest-paid worker in TV. There are people earn-ing £10,000 a time. So I'm doing for peanuts a live show where I could "die" at any minute.' Producer John Fisher outlined his worth. 'The wonderful thing about Terry is his total versatility. He can come on and talk to a soap-opera star and sound just as convincing as though he was tackling a serious issue. There are few people in television capable of doing that. He is always himself. He doesn't become a Parkinson to interview a film star or a Robin Day to talk to a politician. He brings to the chat show a charisma that is unique. He exerts this fascination within the public for wondering how that person is going to react in the presence of Terry Wogan. He does bring a special quality to the show that is difficult to define; others bring it to their own shows but not to he same degree as Terry.' When the portly figure of US gospel singer Jessye Norman left the set to a crash, Wogan didn't hesitate with the line, 'That's Jessye falling over.' The *Wogan* show became famous for its dry ice used for pop performers which lingered in the stage area long after their performance, and of course the ringing telephone backstage, echoing around the Television Theatre.

There was another Royal scoop in July 1986 when the Duke of Edinburgh appeared and revealed the Queen was a backseat driver. He chastised Wogan's use of cue cards, especially one that requested the host to pose a question about the Duke of York's recent wedding. The Duke announced, 'Why don't you hold it up for the audience to look at.' Things went from bad to worse when the Duke was asked if he still held the view that he became more cynical as he got older. This quote had been lifted from an interview a few weeks before and highlighted bad research on the programme as the Duke snapped back, 'Why do you want a secondhand interview. They've all read it if they are interested in *Woman's Own*. Do we have to regurgitate the interview? Can't you think of your own questions?'

The year 1987 saw the show average six million viewers. The show soldiered on, proud that it was one of the very few light-entertainment shows broadcast live. The set changed during this period from 1950s suburban (coffee tables with sputnik legs) to Grecian columns supporting slabs of marble. The format altered with the guests as well: instead of being shunted off after their interview they stayed throughout the programme in the hope they would interact with each other. This became immediately successful when Sarah Keays, Germaine Greer and Marcello Mastroianni made the next day's papers with their scintillating chat. The combination of Lord Soper, Jeffrey Archer and Michael Palin also melded as did a line-up of David Steel, Anne Diamond and Frank Carson. New producer John Fisher advised, 'When you get the chemistry right, the whole is greater than the sum of the parts.'

Fisher was an old hand at chat shows having once been a

producer for the *Parkinson* show. He was adept at pairing guests –
his teaming up of Harold Wilson and Mike Yarwood for *Parkinson*
was a legend in chat-show circles. An author of many books on
vaudeville and showbusiness, Fisher was determined to break
down the watertight compartments into which each Wogan
guest was fitted. 'It comes down to when you're booking a
talk show, you're not just filling chairs. You are going out
to find people with something to say. People worth booking
have got to be worth more than four minutes.' However, the
same old problem of guest availability haunted the show and a
magic mix of chat was not a regular occurrence. Two American
actors that appeared on the show upset the host with their
catatonic attitude. John Malkovich offered a yes-no interlude
which angered Wogan because he felt Malkovich knew exactly
what was expected and led him to think during the interview,
'Why did you come up here?' He was a bit more forgiving to
Anne Bancroft who went to pieces when she discovered the
show was broadcast live.

> *Popularity on television is a paradox. The more people like*
> *you, the more others hate you.*
>
> Terry Wogan

In an article in the *Listener*, David Berry analyzed the appeal of
Terry Wogan: 'It is little wonder, then, that British viewers find
relief in Wogan after the early-evening news, for he is really
saying that things are not so bad, that nothing is too serious to
get in the way of trivia and laughter and entertainment. In an
important sense, Wogan could only be done by an immigrant, by
someone who has not been brought up with the contradictions of
recent British history. Someone who can see from the outside the
desire of the British public to escape from present uncertaintities
back to what made Britain great: the fortitude and modesty of
her people. Only an Irishman could see this and at the same
time, gently mock it in a way which comes across to the British

viewer not as an attack but a celebration. This, then, is Terry Wogan's achievement. In two years he has built a rapport with viewers by confirming our need, amid the challenge of other cultures, to be proud to be British. It is, if nothing else, a distinct achievement.'

Bernard Levin replied to the article in a letter to *The Times*; 'Mr Berry took a long time to pinpoint Wogan's crime, in fact too long. String the bastard up that's what I say; Wogan's popularity and success have clearly been earned by painting a wholly spurious picture of Britain. Nobody but a lunatic would deny that there are many things wrong with this country: sloth, obstinacy and cowardice on both sides of industry, a rising tide of political as well as physical violence and intolerance, a level of public lying for which we would have to go back many decades. Wogan does indeed represent true values, those attitudes, those aspirations which were so politely put down by Mr Berry and which elsewhere, amid foaming hatred, are proclaimed evil. But, in doing so, he is a prophet, and more truly embodies the future of a Britain proud of herself rather than those who declare, with relish, that there is nothing to be proud of in Britain, and that those who feel such pride are enemies of the people.' Wogan had his own opinion: 'To say that we paint too nice a picture, as the *Listener* claimed, is unjustified. When Bernard Levin says I should be strung up he fails to appreciate that the show is screened early in the evening, after the news, and must have elements of light entertainment. I think the British public is intelligent enough to realize what we are doing.' Wogan proved his popularity by winning the *TV Times* Television Personality of the Year award seven times in a row.

> *I get paid a fortune to be mediocre.*
>
> Terry Wogan

Despite constant speculation in the press at the time, no one working on the show ever revealed the backroom secrets of its star and his guests. In February 1988 researcher Mark Georgiou tantalizingly offered a veiled insight into Wogan but offered little in the way of scandal. The host was famed for appearing at planning meetings, puffing on a large cigar and practising his putting in a silk dressing gown. There had been an incident with actor Stewart Granger but he gave no details, and when Ken Dodd appeared an oxygen tent was required backstage, but again no flesh was put on the stories. A long-standing rule of the show of no film clips was broken when Warren Beatty refused to appear without one. After that the ruling was quietly consigned to the dustbin and the clips abounded.

Show 500 was achieved in April 1988, Wogan putting down his longevity to the fact that he had no desk or office at the BBC and was thus able to keep a clear head for his questioning. Mark Lawson of the *Independent* was disconsolate after Barbara Cartland's umpteenth appearance: 'The simple economics of the British chat show are that the demand for guests has always exceeded the supply. Now we have reached a later stage in which the supply of shows excedes the viewer demand.'

George Best's drunken appearance in September 1990 was the series peak as far as press coverage went, followed by a steady decline. Best was in spectacular form. He accused his former Manchester United manager Tommy Docherty of being a bullshitter, and as regards his reputation as a womanizer he told Wogan, 'I like screwing' and spent most of his spare time 'screwing'. England's then manager Graham Taylor was branded a shit and fellow guest Omar Sharif was mauled and interrupted during an anecdote about an actress, with Best annoucing 'she had big tits'. Newspaper switchboards were jammed, with many viewers upset at the complete lack of control exercised by the host which seemed to rankle more than Best's antics.

Despite providing plenty of entertainment for the viewers, Best's appearance fee of £150 was witheld by BBC management in a classic case of understatement as he was judged to have failed to have given a performance. Best had his own slant on his 'performance': 'I get pissed when I feel like getting pissed. My fans were not upset. If they're my fans, they won't be upset. I don't give a fuck what people think. I say what I want to.' The *Guardian* thought that Best should have been in hospital rather than hospitality. Journalist Lester Middlehurst of the now defunct *Today* newspaper speculated that witholding a fee for not giving a performance on *Wogan* was a dangerous precedent to be set by the BBC: 'One would be hard-pushed to remember a guest who lived up to that criterion. They either appear to plug their latest film, book, perfume or record album. Indeed some are wheeled on just to prove that they are still alive.' When actress Bette Davis appeared she seemed bemused by the twenty minutes of polite simpering before declaring, 'Look, I've come on here to sell a book.'

Show one thousand was celebrated with a Madonna interview at her villa in Cannes during the annual film festival. One thousand shows was a major achievement but despite the magnitude of the star the show was an odd celebration. To Madonna this was obviously interview number 63 in a long day and her interviewer some BBC minion who was parked well away from her at the end of the sofa. This was the BBC's major light-entertainment show but somehow that day it had all the atmosphere of a US entertainment magazine slot. Terry looked very nervous and let Madonna fearlessly plug away without interruption. Mark Steyn commented, 'Despite one thousand programmes, in star interviews Terry is like a virgin, as if his kneecap is being touched for the very first time. They're the guests, yet he's the one, awkward and faltering, who doesn't feel at home.'

A trip to New York to interview Arnold Schwarzenegger, Bruce Willis and Sylvester Stallone boosted the ratings but saw Wogan have to suffer the price of such a trio of superstars; the blatant promotion of their restaurant chain, Planet Hollywood. That was the nature of the chat show in the nineties (Michael Aspel would stoop even lower when the threesome appeared on his show). In the same month the show moved from the legendary Television

Theatre (home of everything from *Crackerjack* to *That's Life!*) to Television Centre. In December, Terry Wogan made newspaper history when he became the first TV personality to appear on the front page of the *News of the World* in a story which did not relate to his personal life. The BBC it was revealed were axeing the show in the summer to replace it with a new soap, *Eldorado*. In January 1992 the show got seriously political with four politicians from the same party facing an audience of under 25s, all under the Frost-type supervision of Wogan, who had the look of a man who was there to interview celebrities, not to host *Question Time*.

Humourist Craig Brown aptly summed up the show at the time: 'I am a keen chat-show viewer and I must have watched the Wogan programme at least once a fortnight during its run. This works out at twenty-five Wogans a year for seven years with three guests on each show, making a grand total of at least one hundred and seventy-five Wogans and five hundred and twenty-five guests. Yet however hard I struggle I can't remember a single word spoken on a single show. To be frank, I can't be sure that I remember a single guest.' Wogan appeared eager to get the experience over and done with and fulfil his contract: 'I have been the radio man of the seventies and the TV man of the eighties. Now the question is what do the nineties hold for me? I know you can't sit on top of the Matterhorn for ever. What you have to do is make the slide off the top look imperceptible.'

Guests knew they were in for an easy time on *Wogan* even without the regular host. When Robert Maxwell appeared with Jonathan Ross hosting he ignored completely all questions of financial impropriety and spent his time plugging his newspaper the *European*. Jonathan Ross was dismissed as a threat: 'Jonathan is not so much a rival because the threat to me is me, that I might not do it so well, for two reasons: first, that I might be tired of it and second that the public is tired of my doing it. And perhaps a third, that the BBC is.' Guest hosts on the show included David Frost, Ronnie Corbett, Ben Elton, Clive Anderson, Selina Scott,

Felicity Kendal, Sue Lawley, Kenneth Williams, Anna Ford, Derek Jameson, Esther Rantzen, Mike Smith, Bruce Forsyth, Joanna Lumley and Jonathan Ross. Wogan accepted that some criticism was justified but stressed that he was not an interviewer in the mould of Brian Walden, with his confrontational style: 'That is his field of expertise. Mine is perhaps shallower but it is no less valid. And I never let anyone see they have upset me. The whole game is about masking your feelings. Some people say that in life you should let your feelings out. I believe they should be controlled. I am a typical Irishman. I want to please. I don't show anger. One of the major faults in our whole life is selfishness. When I hear of men wanting to leave their wives because they want to find themselves I feel like throwing up.'

The *Observer* observed, 'A common complaint about Wogan is that he is bland, but that is to miss the point. He is simply a consummate professional who recognised from the outset that blandness is a sine qua non for a popular chat show in a country like Britain.' When Michelle Pfeiffer appeared on one of the last-ever shows to promote her role as Catwoman in *Batman Returns* the whole essence of *Wogan* and indeed Eamonn Andrews before him was captured. Pfeiffer's role and costume hinted at a dark, S&M side to her personality but Wogan kicked off with, 'Why would anybody want to get into a role where they dressed up in black plastic?' An amazed Pfeiffer had to set her host right, 'It was rubber.'

> It's not the end of the world – it's only telly.
>
> Terry Wogan

The series reached the end of the road on 3 July 1992, after seven and a half years and about three thousand guests, with a compendium of greatest moments. In the world of showbiz the word Wogan had become a new term as in 'doing Wogan' or 'we're hoping for Wogan'. As the series came to an end Terry told the *Radio Times*, 'Seven and a half years. They said it would collapse after six weeks. I think there's a law of diminishing returns. People get sick of the sight of you.' As Wogan said, 'You don't have to be a journalist to conduct these interviews. The most successful ones are just fooling around.' To his credit Wogan recognized his time was up and was willing to scrap the show that bore his name at the expense of his £500,000 salary: 'I've been at the cutting edge for seven years and I know if you don't change, you're going to be left behind.'

Wogan had been keen to leave the studio and conduct interviews in Hollywood but the idea had been rejected by the BBC. An experimental trip had been tried but attracted only Zsa Zsa Gabor, George Burns and Bob Hope. Meanwhile Michael Aspel's forays to the US had attracted contemporary talent and thus a much younger viewer. Wogan wrote his own epitaph for his show: 'One thing is certain, that I am not going to last as long as Johnny Carson did in America with a chat show for twenty-five years. Television hasn't got any better, it has only got quicker. Television goes in one eye and out the other. No one in our business is going to leave footprints in the sands of time.'

The spring of 1996 found Wogan a less than ubiquitous presence on television with only one series, *Auntie's Bloomers*, providing a regular slot. He still hosted *Eurovision* and *Children In Need* but his Radio 2 morning slot was his main broadcasting outlet. Terry Wogan is dismissive of past accusations of blandness against his chat show: 'Well it was a talk show not an in-depth interview and there aren't any good ones now, here or in America. David Letterman just wouldn't be tolerated here, he's so trivial. I saw him interview a singer recently. 'How ya doin'?' he said as he greeted her. 'How ya doin'?' he repeated as he hugged her, and when she sat down, 'How ya doin'?' This is the man who is extolled. Come on. It drove me mad when I was compared with people who did a recorded talk show once a week.'

He still, however, hankered for the magical five-nights-a-week chat-show slot which had been denied to both him and the BBC hierarchy: 'I wouldn't mind doing a TV talk show again, although it would have to be five nights a week, and late. But I don't think anyone would ask me, any more than they'd ask Michael Parkinson, because I'm an old geezer. There are new people and that's the way it should be.'

LARRY KING

CNN launched *Larry King Live* on 3 June 1985. With his swept-back hair, bright-red braces and rolled-up shirtsleeves, King looked every inch a hard-nosed reporter from a Hollywood film settling down to pen tomorrow's front page. Turning on CNN any day of the week viewers would be constantly amazed at the calibre of the guests on the other side of King's desk, from presidents to reclusive film stars. No one else in the field of talk shows could claim guests of the calibre of Margaret Thatcher, Marlon Brando, Mikhail Gorbachev and Barbra Streisand. The hard-boiled image of King however is merely a façade. Often branded as 'The King of Schmooze', the key word for *Larry King Live* is congeniality.

Politicians and celebrities love the show as it rarely amounts to more than a cosy chat. Ex-President Richard Nixon must have been delighted with his appearance in 1992 when the subject of Watergate was raised only once. King merely asked, 'Is it hard to drive by the Watergate?' to which Nixon replied, 'Well, I've never been in the Watergate.' From King, 'Never been in?' 'No,' replied Nixon and the conversation moved on. His consistent run of interviews with eccentric billionaire Ross Perot gave him the most successful run for a third-party presidential candidate in 80 years. More a meeting of old friends than a serious debating forum King remains after ten years the major outlet for newsmakers. He denies any complicity with guests to make things easy. 'I like questions that begin with "why" and "how" and I listen to the answers, which leads to more questions.' King's flamboyance off screen attracts interest as much as on. Married many times, he is rarely out of the gossip columns and with the help of CNN has become one of the most recognized faces on television around the world.

Born Larry Zeigler in Brooklyn in 1933 he developed a lifelong love of radio, sports and newspapers as a child. In the late 1950s he made his radio debut in Miami after sweeping the floors at the station and adopted the surname King. Successful as a DJ he began hosting a talking show from a popular Miami restaurant interviewing people right across the social spectrum from waitresses to union leader Jimmy Hoffa and comedian Lenny Bruce. This grounding proved invaluable for his future career. 'I had an ability to draw people out in an interview. The key to my success as an interviewer is in the fact that I am truly interested in a person's craft, in his or her work.'

With television appearances and a gossip column in a news-paper King fast became the social hub of Miami. He became close friends with multi-millionaire Lou Wolfson who bankrolled some talk-show pilots for King which came to nothing. When Wolfson faced trial for financial irregularities King convinced him to allow him funds to use the best attorneys available. King, however, siphoned off part of the proceeds to rescue himself from his own precarious financial situation. He confessed all to Wolfson who promptly had him charged with theft but, after long court delays, King managed to escape trial and the charges were dropped. By the 1970s he had all but dropped out of any media activities, leading instead a hedonistic lifestyle revolving around women and sport. He returned to radio and station WIOD where he began his restaurant career in 1975 and once more took up his newspaper duties. Despite returning to journalistic activities the lure of gambling did not die and King was declared bankrupt in 1978.

He doesn't try to embarrass anybody or put anybody on the spot. I was glad I'd found a new friend.

Nancy Reagan

A late-night radio talk show, the *Larry King Show*, was launched in that year. During his years in the social whirl King had picked up an impressive array of contacts and the show played host to major names like Frank Sinatra and former President Gerald Ford. The show proved to be the model for *Larry King Live*. With no prior research or meeting with his guest, King would question them spontaneously and then throw open the phone lines to the audience. After this King conducted a general phone-in where listeners could talk about any subject. The show entered syndication and was soon heard right across America by a devoted audience. He moved the format into television in 1983 and CNN signed him for *Larry King Live* in 1985. The show stands alone in the US talk-show pantheon. If someone appears promoting a book, King won't have read it – 'I want to start even with the listener,' he says. His relaxed style frustrates many of his CNN colleagues but he emanates a complete lack of concern to all criticism.

The power of the show was underlined in 1993 when an alleged expert David Reynard claimed, with no medical evidence, that cellular phones had caused his wife's death from brain cancer. King précised the show with the announcement, 'Some say cellular phones can kill you'. Many callers claimed they suffered from headaches when using mobile phones. Cellular company stocks dropped overnight as government and industry officials attempted to right the situation based on speculation. A judge later threw out Reynard's damages claim. After the O.J. Simpson verdict there was only one place for Simpson to argue his case and that was *Larry King Live*. He didn't appear in the studio but rang in to challenge some points about the verdict and its subsequent treatment on television. His opinion was heard across the world without risk of trial by television.

Part of King's skill is treating his telephone callers with respect. They are not merely cheap appendages, filling out time. He sees their questions as every bit as important as his. With CNN's world reach his show is truly part of the global village, with calls from Arkansas to Amsterdam. Many guests refused to appear in the early years because of the uncertainty of the phone calls. King suffered a massive heart-attack in 1987 and underwent quintuple-bypass surgery. He quit smoking and toned down his classic hard-living newsman's lifestyle, married again and returned to the hot seat.

> *Larry King liberated me by giving me to the American people directly.*
>
> President Clinton

King's rapport with politicians, especially the most powerful, saw him starstruck from the beginning of his career. In the 1960s he told presidential candidate Adlai Stevenson, 'To be in your presence is a singular honour.' Martin Luther King and Bobby Kennedy all passed through as did the three 1968 presidential candidates, Richard Nixon, George Wallace and Hubert Humphrey. When Bill Clinton and his running mate Al Gore appeared on *Larry King Live* things were totally relaxed. Clinton's mother rang in to say hello. In a later show with Gore his wife rang in anonymously and propositioned him on air. When George Bush was president he conquered his aversion to talk shows to enjoy questions like, 'Do you think you're getting a bad rap?' and, 'When was the last time you drove?' Bush was delighted to reach in his pocket and show King his driver's licence. *Larry King Live* became the most pre-eminent show in the political arena. President Clinton admitted his regular appearances almost negated his need for holding formal press conferences. Even someone as notoriously publicity shy as David Letterman appeared for a relaxed one-to-one. Letterman was so relaxed he instantly agreed with a caller to change the famous host city of his Top Ten Lists from Sioux City, Iowa to Grand Rapids, Michigan.

However, by the mid 1990s ratings began to slump with King appearing to tread water. A 1995 interview with Clinton and Gore was so lacklustre it was only enlivened by the president's Marlon Brando impersonation. King still holds the crown and continues to host the talk show everyone is happy to appear on.

JONATHAN ROSS

The Last Resort, *a show which generally speaking has all
the wit and charm of a vandalised public urinal.*
                                        Michael Parkinson

All British chat shows are indebted to the US format but Jonathan
Ross and *The Last Resort* was the first to use a host who performed
as much as his guests, much in the manner of Steve Allen
and David Letterman. *The Last Resort* could have easily been
renamed 'Late Night with Ross' such was its debt to that
show, but its distillation of the concept to suit British tastes
worked wonderfully well over two series and made its host a
household name.

Ross graduated, bizarrely, with a history degree from the
School of Slavonic and East European Studies. A student without
a job, he was £400 in debt and about to become a security man
before trying his luck in television (where he had previously
worked as a child actor in adverts for Persil and Rice Krispies).
He was involved with Channel 4 from its inception, working as
a researcher on early shows such as *Solid Soul, Soul Train* and
the famously inept *Loose Talk*. He formulated the idea of *The Last
Resort* with *Solid Soul* producer Alan Marke, astutely forming a
production company (Channel X) to sell the whole package to
Channel 4. He secretly harboured ambitions to host the show and

when auditions failed to deliver a suitable presenter he gratefully accepted the role: 'Everyone was hoping that I would, only I was too embarrassed to suggest it.'

The whole concept was very much based on all-round entertainment rather than a slick host gamely bantering with his guests: 'I got the idea after seeing Kenneth Williams trotted out as a chat-show guest for about the four hundredth time. It was boring and there was nothing to interest my age group. I deliberately want to get away from the chat-show bullshit of saying someone's book was wonderful. I'm looking for a person who has made a lousy film and I'll say the film's crap, but in a light way, not a horrible way.' The show became the first UK chat show to utilize a hip house band as opposed to the usual staid musical director beloved of *Parkinson* and *Wogan*. Elvis Costello cohort Steve Nieve and the Playboys brought the US flavour of a tight bunch of musicians who could perform anything to order and were not merely appendages governed by musical notation strictly adhered to. Indeed, Paul McCartney performed with them early on in the series, his first live TV session in many years.

> *We are the Carry On of chat shows.*
>> Jonathan Ross

> *Untalented rubbish.*
>> The Guardian

Ross's brief was simple when the show first aired on 9 January 1987: 'To begin with none of the guests will be allowed to shamelessly plug their new books or films. If they try I'll divert them into discussions about their murky pasts or their early haircuts. Take Donald Sutherland. We've got him on early in the series and he's got a shocking haircut history. That dreadful perm in *Invasion of the Body Snatchers* is something he should be accountable for. I paid good money to see that movie!' Channel 4 were sold the idea as a comedy show in the format of a chat show. The first series used wrestler Mick McManus as a referee to keep the guests in order. Cult figures from the past were utilized; Donny Osmond emerged from 1980s obscurity to perform 'Puppy Love', backed by Hank Wangford and Billy Bragg.

Show one set the standard with Page 3 girl Maria Whittaker as a guest. Ross knew, as did the viewing audience, that chat would not be her forte so she donned a blindfold and gave her opinion on a selection of chocolate mousses. 'I went to meet her and thought I could be in trouble, what do I do with her. In many ways it was indefensible. I presented her as a dumb sex-object, but then she is a sex-object, I certainly fancied her.' Ross's skill was outlined by his attitude with the guest: she was in on the joke and was not denigrated by her appearance. Ross was completely at home with his star guests and was certainly not in awe of them. Sean Connery was challenged about his hair: 'I suppose if you had a decent rug sorted out it would be okay.' Actor Timothy Spall was introduced by Ross with little preamble: 'You've played a lot of fat slobs.' Boxer Joe Bugner was interviewed by Ross with the host playing dumb, thinking he was interviewing Frank Bruno. Paul McCartney agreed to appear because he was a big fan of the show: 'He told me the fascination was that there was one very thin idea each week taken to ridiculous extremes.' When Tom Jones appeared on the show, Ross had no qualms in joining him to sing 'It's Not Unusual' and single-handedly made the ageing star a once-more credible item.

When his conversation with Jerry Hall lacked punch he challenged her to a leg wrestling challenge, a sport he had noted in his research notes she had enjoyed as a child in Texas. The show hit the headlines however with the appearance of an illusionist who swallowed a length of string and then appeared to extract the blood-soaked item from his stomach. Lacking all the pretensions of standard British stage magicians, the illusion and its presentation on the show gave the all-important impression that it was all real, with Ross appearing as appalled as the audience. The whole idea was to be the opposite of the sanitized British chat show. Oliver Reed's drunken performance on *Aspel & Co.* would have been handled differently on *The Last Resort*. Ross speculated that he would have acknowledged Reed's drunkenness instantly by conducting his interview at a bar, testing cocktails being served by the barman of the year. When actor Harry Dean Stanton appeared on the show much the worse for wear, Ross managed to keep things bubbling even when Stanton threatened to attack an acid-house party organizer with violence after being chained to his seat.

Ross opines, 'They're always in seats. I can't do that. I sit behind a desk to talk to people. I do try to keep my opinions to myself, keeping politics and things out largely, but there are things we won't do. We won't humiliate people. We had an old guy on with an electric suit, and before he went on I said, "You realise that people are going to laugh at you for being eccentric" but he said that was fine. People like that I won't try and be hard on but with someone like Boy George I know he's going to give as good as he gets so we can play around a bit more.' What set Ross apart from his contemporaries, his youth aside, was his total hands-on approach to the show. There were no rehearsals in silk dressing gowns for him or a snatched conversation with a researcher before showtime. He worked full days with the production team and did his own research with guests well before the programme: 'Everyone's opinion is as valid as mine it's just nowhere near as important.'

The press liked the format. Andrew Hislop of *The Times*: 'The cocky charm of the callow chat-show host Ross is a curious mixture of style-generation cool and straining for laughs mania, as though the stripped-to-his-pants kid from the launderette Levis ad had metamorphosed into Danny Kaye.' The show started to hit the headlines as guests began to misbehave. Dawn French admitted she was becoming 'moist' at the thought that Tom Jones was about to sing and when film director Terry

Gilliam came on as the next guest he made a big performance of sniffing the former guest's chair. Steve Martin appeared on the show (after seeing a tape of the show which he thought was awful) performing his Great Flydini sketch, producing items out of his flies, and Ross was amazed that people asked him where he found such a great comedian. Martin was a major star in the US but more of a cult figure here through his early films (although he had made a *Parkinson* appearance early on in his career), and *The Last Resort* was the only TV vehicle at the time where his unique talent could be displayed. Roland Rivron in his Dr Scrote mode dispensed advice while Joey the Parrot became a co-host. Ross interviewed EastEnder Wendy Richards whilst wearing Mickey Mouse ears.

Channel 4 increased the initial run from ten to fifteen and moved the show from its midnight slot to 10.30 p.m. In the spirit of the string illusion, regurgitator Stevie Starr became a regular, bringing up everything from coins to goldfish. Ross was dismissive of his rivals: 'Wogan is a bit childish, all that stuff about the old tummy spreading. He's got a stock set of mannerisms and jokes that he relies on. Parkinson made a mistake in coming back. I genuinely think he's talked out, he has nothing new to ask people, he's had them all before. Harty's show is one I've never really watched. I thought he was always a bit too affected and went after wacky people all the time.' Jaci Stephen in the *Evening Standard* heaped praise on the show: 'Apologies to all those who write demanding that the filth be attacked but to me *The Last Resort* is the funniest, most entertaining and most successful chat-show on television.'

Ross was an immediate success as a personality, much like David Frost before him and, in the same mould, was a shrewd financial operator. Being put in the same bracket as Frost irked Ross: 'There's no comparison, Frost was probing, confrontational. *The Last Resort* seeks to entertain not inform. I'm not particularly good at being a chat-show host but I think I'm really good at being silly on screen, that's what the show is about. The joy

comes from me being silly with a guest you might think is too
big to be fooled around with like Tom Jones or Sean Connery'.
A headline in 1987 christened him 'The Modern Media Man'
in a story that had him turning down a six-figure fee for an
advert. Ross would later score a major coup when he fronted
a series of ads for Harp lager and appeared as a *TV Times* cover
star with the product clearly in view on his desk. An approach
by London Weekend to host a satire show was rebuffed after
he demanded a salary of half a million. London Weekend head
Greg Dyke admitted that no one on their roster was paid that
sort of money. He cockily turned down a Terry Wogan stand-in
slot (but later took up the challenge). The BBC also failed to lure
him with an offer to revive the ancient *Sunday Night at the London
Palladium* slot Beat the Clock for *Seaside Special*.

He remained with Channel 4 with a re-jigged chat show,
One Hour with Jonathan Ross, which included a current-affairs
discussion alongside a game show, *Knock Down Ginger*. He
later made a series on cult films and film-makers called *The
Incredibly Strange Picture Show*. By 1990 he succumbed to the
lure of *Wogan*, filling in for two weeks to improve, as he said,
'the programme's dress sense'. He explained that he wanted to
try the mainstream: 'I couldn't do a po-faced interview if I tried.
I'm best at high-speed comic interviews with my tongue firmly
in my cheek, that's my way.' The *One Hour* was a flop, lacking
the spark of *The Last Resort* and his star waned slightly when the
BBC gave Sue Lawley the job as Wogan's number one deputy.

> *I don't regard Jonathan Ross as a rival. He was over-hyped
> and the show didn't deliver. He was interviewing people we
> had done weeks before.*
>
>   Terry Wogan

Channel 4 tried again in the autumn of 1990 with a thrice-weekly
chat show, *Tonight with Jonathan Ross*. Broadcast at 6.30 p.m. on
'Wogan nights', Monday, Wednesday and Friday, the show was
not a success. Within six months the viewing figures had barely

touched 1.6 million against the modest target of two million that Channel 4 had set. Ironically, the man who had provided an alternative to the anodyne chat-show formula had failed to usurp Wogan's crown and had been reduced to interviewing less than stellar guests: his first had been snooker player John Parrott. There were a few highs such as Mel Gibson and Audrey Hepburn but Channel X partner Alan Marke admitted that, after ITV and BBC, 'we get the scrapings'.

By 1990 Channel X was turning over close to three million pounds a year with its wide range of programmes which included Vic Reeves' and Bob Mortimer's show. Ross explained the key to all the shows he worked on was that the air of shambolic chaos masked plenty of rehearsal. He was less than modest when asked if he was giving up interviewing: 'Yes but not in the immediate future. Firstly because I enjoy it and secondly, because not a lot of people can do it as well as I can. There's a short shelf-life in this job, so you've got to push yourself. It is really very simple. A lot of television people pretend it's much more difficult than it is, but there are lots of martyrs in this business. People take themselves too seriously, I don't know why, it's only television.' A major plus as host of *Wogan* was to persuade Madonna to fly to Britain for an interview. Ross seemed happy to settle into a standard showbiz role with run-of-the-mill shows like *Gag Tag*, *Fantastic Facts* and *Saturday Zoo*.

The dangerous element still exists when he acts as a live host and delivers some stinging comedy. His Mondo Rosso show on strange film genres showed that he had lost nothing of his cheeky interviewing style. Now signed with LWT he hosts one-off documentaries, titled *In Search of . . .*, profiling such subjects as James Bond or Dracula. The summer of 1996 saw him taking on the Hughie Green-style role as host of the talent programme *The Big Big Talent Show* which was back for a second run in 1997.

ARSENIO HALL

No one put the late-night silver spoon in my mouth.
                                                    Arsenio Hall

Although his shows came nowhere near the greats of the US chat-show hierachy, Arsenio Hall deserves his place in history as the man who caused a shift away from the showbusiness establishment of stars to younger, hipper guests and a cooler, more laconic approach to the art of chat. Debuting in January 1989 his show had a party atmosphere. The audience whooped and whooped as the designer-clad host strutted the stage and interviewed the hottest young film and pop stars. Not least when President Clinton appeared on the show to play saxophone. Carson and the whole *Tonight Show* culture looked anachronistic alongside and the ratings soared. Guests ranged from rapper Ice-T to sex therapist Dr Ruth Westeheimer. She was asked by Hall if she had ever faked orgasm whilst he ploughed straight into Brooke Shields asking her to confirm the long-publicized state of her virginity. With the continual 'high fives' and an audience wound up to maximum adulation, Hall's show was an immediate hit.

Born in Cleveland in 1955, the son of a Baptist minister, he spent his childhood worshipping Carson (he even learnt to play drums like his idol) and other talk-show hosts. He graduated from

Kent State University, Cleveland, in 1977 and settled down to a career in pharmaceuticals. Inspired one night whilst watching the *Tonight Show* he decided to quit and enter comedy full time, following in the footsteps of many a chat-show host before him. Moving to Chicago he overcame severe stage fright and became popular in stand-up.

By 1979 he had broken into the fringes of show business working as a comedy warm-up man for various acts on the road that included Aretha Franklin, Neil Sedaka and Patrice Rushen. A stint with Nancy Wilson resulted in her encouraging him to make his fortune in Los Angeles. He soon began opening for stars of the calibre of Tom Jones and Tina Turner and became a regular at the Comedy Store where he formed a lifelong friendship with Eddie Murphy. Turned down at an audition for the *Tonight Show* because his humour was considered too college-based, he found a mentor in singer Patti Labelle. She allowed him to perform edgier material before her shows rather than the more conservative form of comedy he had used for other singers.

Television beckoned with the *½ Hour Comedy Hour*, a short-lived summer show in 1983, followed by a regular slot on *Thicke of the Night*, a talk show hosted by Alan Thicke. He appeared on *Motown Revue*, the music show *Solid Gold* and became a voice on the kid's cartoon series *The Real Ghostbusters*. He finally made it onto the *Tonight Show* in 1986, albeit when Carson's seat was being subbed by Joan Rivers. His break came when Fox needed someone to fill in on the *Joan Rivers Show* after her dismissal. Hall had been a hit as a guest on the show and as he picked up his dry-cleaning one day in August 1987 he received a call from his manager asking if he could deputize on the show as host. He simply donned his newly clean suit, drove to the studio, took over the reins and became an overnight hit. He rode out the last eleven weeks of Joan River's contract at $1,000 a night.

He immediately used that three-month period to create what he had always wanted to do: 'I figured I'd make a show for people who just didn't relate to the kind of show Carson's doing.' He had measured the audience's needs almost perfectly. The 90-minute show had all the atmosphere of a gospel meeting with the audience cheering Hall's every move. Eddie Murphy was a regular alongside Mike Tyson and other major black stars. Groups outside the musical mainstream were regular fixtures and the show struck an instant bond with its audience. Committed to launching a new show without Hall when his run had finished, Fox had to face the wrath of Hall fans when the series ended and they instantly aired re-runs. Realizing they had one of TV's hottest properties, Fox offered him a deal for his own show but the wise Hall angled for a syndication-styled agreement which Fox rejected. Paramount stepped in with a deal for both film and TV work and a new star of late night was born.

Co-starring with Eddie Murphy in the film *Coming to America* made him instantly and internationally known as the film became a worldwide hit. Contractual problems prevented the launch of his chat show for a year and during this period self-doubt crept in as to whether he could carry a talk show night after night. An appearance on the *Tonight Show* in July 1988 soon dispelled the gloom when Hall and Carson entertained the audience with magic tricks in the commercial breaks: 'It was being out there that had made me realize I was about to compromise my dream. I said the hell with "too hard". All my life, I've wanted to do what this man does.' Hall created his show from scratch, designing the set, penning the theme and writing his own monologues. The *Arsenio Hall Show* soon attracted guests of the calibre of Madonna and Roseanne Barr as its rating began to grow. As one critic described it, 'The show is hip, hipper than anything else on late-night TV.' The style element of the show was the main ingredient.

Guests knew they wouldn't be getting a rough ride on the Hall sofa, it was all adoration and saccharine-laden questions. As Hall explained, 'I'm throwing a party on my show. And when you invite people over for a party, you don't cross-examine them.' This formula was obviously hot, as a 1991 *Time*/CNN poll revealed that Hall was the most popular host on late-night television. He said at the time, 'I just ask what y'all are thinking anyway. When I'm on the air, if I'm too worried about ratings or bookings, that takes you out of the game. You miss an obvious follow-up question. I don't want to have background research cards. That takes away from the ability to have a real conversation. You can't listen with cards. Unlike most talk shows, on my show the audience in a sense becomes the co-host of a late-night party. They are to me what Ed McMahon was to Johnny Carson. My philosophy is to leave my ego at the door and get the best out of my guests. That TV set is my place. I invite you to it and I'm a nice host. I'm here to entertain and to treat you like I would if you were in my home.'

The revivalist atmosphere of the audience gave the show an edge as the audience reacted loudly to every nuance of the host and his guests. One-on-one basketball competitions were common, giving the impression of a bunch of guys hanging out on a street corner. Guests joined in the fun: Mike Tyson, Magic Johnson and Emma Samms sang 'When the Saints Go Marching In' with Little Richard. Madonna took exception to Hall's teasing about her hairdo. He dismissed her with the line, 'She has borrowed our sound but not our sensibilities.' In April 1992 Hall took a step to quell the LA riots by inviting the mayor, Tom Bradley, on the show to appeal for calm. Hall was a man in constant motion offstage and on: 'I change every day. One day I have a heart of gold, the next day I want to march with Al Sharpton the rest of my life. I'm America's most schizophrenic entertainer. I never want to allow myself to get comfortable. I was born to do this. When I'm in the spotlight I'm gone. I love it more than anything in the world. When everyone is barking and screaming it's the best feeling I've ever felt, like a three-point jumper with one second left in the championship game against Boston, better than an orgasm.'

His salary soon exceed $12 million a year but his rise to the stellar heights was being eclipsed. His star was already fading as the short attention span of his young audience moved elsewhere. The launch of *Leno vs. Letterman* in the autumn of 1992 saw viewers reaching for their channel changers as the massive publicity for the Lords of Late Night dominated the media. Helen Kushnick, the *Tonight Show* producer of the Jay Leno-fronted programme, also conspired against him. In her war over keeping guests loyal to that show it was rumoured that Kushnick had told her staff that they had the power to kill the *Arsenio Hall Show* and remove it from the air. Hall openly attacked the *Tonight Show* in *Entertainment Weekly* claiming he would 'kick Jay's ass in the ratings'. Former *Tonight Show* alumi Ed McMahon and Doc Severinsen appeared on the show to trash the *Tonight Show* much to Hall's delight. However, as the late-night market expanded to take on even more shows Hall suffered and his show was discarded as Leno and Letterman forged on.

JAY LENO

*When I finish my act, I go back to my room and watch
television, or I'll go out for pizza with a friend. I'm hopelessly
American. If something doesn't come in a Styrofoam box
with a lid on it, I'm lost.*

Jay Leno

Jay Leno is the talk-show host who took over the toughest job
in showbusiness. The burly, lantern jawed (he is the man for
whom the adjective was created) comedian had to fill the shoes
of the man who most of the American population regarded as the
personification of the genre, Johnny Carson. Leno's attributes
as a comedian were unique. He doesn't drink, smoke, take
drugs or chase women. He never uses blue humour and is
a happily married man. The *Hollywood Reporter* described him
thus, 'Jay Leno is schtickless. He is not neurotic, self-deprecating,
crazed or raunchy. He doesn't pace across stage, scream like
a banshee or deliver his lines in a monotone stupor and he
doesn't play the accordion. The guy is just plain funny.' When
the candidates for the *Tonight Show* host narrowed down to just
Leno and Letterman there could be no doubt who was most
in the Carson mould. Leno has the ability to adapt current
events and extract gentle humour from it, whilst Letterman's
brand of sarcasm provided a slightly hard, New York edge.

With Leno the transition between old and new was almost seamless.

> *I come to work and everybody applauds. My life's a vacation.*
>
> Jay Leno

Born in New York in 1950, Leno is unique amongst the most successful chat-show hosts having carved his career entirely from being a comedian. He didn't serve any form of television apprenticeship at a remote TV station in the US Midwest. Comedy, its essence and construction, has been the major motivating force of his life since he first took the stage. At junior school during a class discussion about Robin Hood a teacher told the pupils that people were killed at that time by being boiled in oil. Leno raised his hand, 'But they couldn't boil Tuck.' Pause. 'He was a friar.' As he recalls, 'That was the first time I think I ever told a joke joke, a grown-up joke. And I remember thinking, "Hmmm, that's an interesting reaction". And since then I've always been able to remember everything I said, good or bad, and the reaction it got. I was never particularly good at remembering names or spelling or adding, but I could always remember what made people laugh.'

Graduating from college in 1973 with a degree in speech therapy, Leno found work as a mechanic for Rolls-Royce and other such luxury cars. He had already worked in stand-up in Boston and now began to venture into New York to try the comic scene there. An appearance by a comedian on the *Tonight Show* decided him for a career in showbusiness. He felt his act was far better than the one he saw and so decided to uproot and move to California to try to break the big time. Leno claims he told his neighbours to take anything they wanted from his apartment, packed a flight bag and took the overnight flight to Los Angeles. He played the Los Angeles club circuit and found work as a gag writer for comedy star Jimmie Walker then appearing in the TV sitcom *Good Times*. Leno would later pass this job on to David Letterman after they had met at the Comedy Club. Letterman is fulsome in his praise of Leno at that time: 'He was head and shoulders above anybody else. I patterned much of what I did on what I saw him do. It's no surprise to any of us that he's gotten so successful. I think everybody was surprised that it took him a little longer. The first night I saw him, I thought the next day he was going to be a huge star.' Leno was equally impressed with Letterman's deadpan material and delivery.

In 1975 Johnny Carson saw Leno's act at the Improv Club on the recommendation of a *Tonight Show* talent booker. He spoke to the budding comedian, briefly advising him to cut the stories in his routines and concentrate on the jokes. A disappointed Leno later admitted he sought out Carson's car in the car park and pelted it with eggs. However, after studying the *Tonight Show* he realized Carson was right, delivering fifteen to twenty jokes in the time it took him to deliver four or five. That year saw Leno becoming a regular on the talk shows of Merv Griffin, Dinah Shore and Mike Douglas. After a tip-off from Steve Martin he finally made it on to the *Tonight Show* on 2 March 1977. Leno categorized his appearance: 'Your first *Tonight Show* is kind of like your first girl. I mean, it's real fast. It's over real quick. You weren't very good. But you never forget it. But you do know you want to do it again. And do it better the next time.'

He followed up with a few more appearances but a lack of new material saw the *Tonight Show* lose interest. It was another eight years before he secured a slot on the show. He decided to go back on the road to sharpen up his routines and became a cast member on the *Marilyn McCoo and Billy Davis Jr Show*. He also appeared in a number of films such as *Fun with Dick and Jane*, *Silver Bears*, *American Hot Wax* and *Americathon*. He found popularity on the nightclub circuit, opening for Johnny Mathis, Tom Jones, Perry Como and John Denver. Leno's long, hard years on the road paid off as he built a reputation with a gruelling schedule but his lack of a major TV role held him back. Almost overnight he saw contemporaries such as Billy Crystal, Robin Williams and of course David Letterman all become stars. His looks didn't help: many producers turned him down, bluntly claiming he was too ugly.

> *I'm sure if you caught him at some unguarded moment, you would see a panel fall open on his chest to reveal wires and electrodes. He is Robocomic.*
>
> Jerry Seinfeld

By the beginning of the 1980s he had married and settled down to an affluent lifestyle in the Hollywood Hills. When *Late Night with Letterman* hit the air in 1982 Leno became a regular guest on the show, his comedy becoming spontaneous with his old friend far more than it had with elder statesman Johnny Carson. He made his *Late Show* debut on 15 April 1982 on a show which included an elevator races competition. He delivered a first-rate stand-up show and then interacted with Letterman in a fast-paced conversation. Leno remarked, 'The show is geared well to what I do, in the sense that a lot of jokes I do there wouldn't work on other shows, because the host wouldn't have the rapport I have with David and wouldn't know what I'm talking about.'

The year 1986 saw his breakthrough as he worked over 300 club and cabaret dates and at last made a major impact on television hosting *Saturday Night Live* and appearing in the special *Jay Leno and the American Dream*. Like Letterman before him, NBC recognized a major talent and signed him to a retaining contract with no specific show. When Joan Rivers quit the *Tonight Show* to go to Fox he became permanent guest host alongside Garry Shandling and discovered he was far more relaxed delivering a monologue and merely reacting to guests rather than having to provide a constant fount of comedy. He never used research notes but always reacted spontaneously with his guests. By the end of the eighties he was a major showbiz earner, averaging $25,000 to $30,000 a performance.

Shortly before Carson announced his retirement in 1991 the *New York Post* ran a story that Leno had the job ahead of Letterman. Carson's 'no comment' on a successor led to massive speculation in the TV industry over who would get the job. Whilst on his tours Leno had always agreed to appear on NBC-affiliated TV stations to record promos for them, so he was immediately in favour, backed by his sterling work as guest host. As he commented, 'I've played every city in the country including Alaska at least once. I've worked with network affiliates, giving interviews, helping them do spots, selling tickets. I think I have them to thank.' Leno was typically downbeat when told he had the gig: 'This is a job I always wanted, that I thought it would be neat to have.' Perhaps a more prosaic reason was that Letterman's style just wouldn't have washed with the conservative *Tonight Show* audience. Letterman always tore into any guest celebrity or civilian who missed the plot. Leno was more gentle, targetting only the rich and famous. He was the perfect dividing line between old-style Carson showbiz and Letterman anti-showbiz.

> *The real trick in this town is to make showbusiness money and live like a normal person.*
>
> Jay Leno

Monday, 25 May 1992 saw the debut of the *Tonight Show* with Jay Leno and a new era. Carson had broadcast his last show the Friday before but all the remnants of his 30-year reign had disappeared as Leno stepped forward to deliver the monologue. The Ed McMahon-style sidekick was gone, as was the big-band sound of Doc Severinsen, replaced by the ultra-cool jazz of Branford Marsalis. Leno's long-time manager, Helen Kushnick, took over as executive producer. As that first show came to an end, Leno confidently asserted himself with, 'Not bad if I do say so myself.' Throughout that initial show Leno made no reference whatsoever to Johnny Carson, despite numerous feeds from guest Billy Crystal. Many at NBC found this ungracious. Leno told *Rolling Stone* years later, 'I take complete credit for not doing it. It was the biggest mistake I ever made.'

However, the first few months were rocky with Leno falling over himself in order to appeal to the *Tonight Show* audience. Leno found it a major leap, switching from guest to permanent host. The monologue had to be churned out every night to reflect the topical issues of the day. Jeff Jarvis of *TV Guide* thought that Leno was 'acting like a puppy in need of a tummy scratch' and that when he told jokes 'he steps over his punchlines and pleads for laughs with practiced sheepishness and aren't-I-cute grins'. Despite the creaky beginnings the *Tonight Show* ratings bore up.

Rumours were also spreading over Hollywood that rival shows were suffering from an anonymous edict that guests appearing on shows other than the *Tonight Show* would not be welcome opposite Leno. This was proven true when country star Travis Tritt's manager Ken Kragen went public and claimed Tritt had been told that, if he appeared on the rival *Arsenio Hall Show*, he could forget a *Tonight Show* appearance. The same scenario was claimed for another Kragen act, Trisha Yearwood. Helen Kushnick vehemently denied the claims and said, 'I've upset the balance of power. They don't want a woman doing this.' Kushnick had become the autocratic ruler of the *Tonight Show*, hiring and firing at will. Network executives stood back in amazement as she pulled a *Tonight Show* from the air after coverage of the Republican Convention was extended. The audience was sent home and the set put into darkness. NBC hurriedly aired a repeat with many in the television industry expressing their concern that a producer could hold a network hostage. Kushnick was later relieved of her production duties but Leno stuck by her, claiming, 'They should come after me, that's what this job is about. Would I be lazy if there weren't other talk shows, you bet.'

Leno began to refine his interviewing craft: 'I think that as TV enters the nineties, people would rather watch somebody with an opinion, even if they don't agree with it. We've reached a point where PR has become such a science that when people are pushing something, they know exactly what to say to hype it. When you get somebody with an honest opinion then it makes the talk real.' Unlike Letterman he never struck an attitude with difficult guests and in some cases was wholesomely naive. He asked homosexual playwright Harvey Fierstein about his lifestyle, innocently delivering the line, 'I don't mean to be odd, but what's a gay guy's opening?' As he explained, 'I was being totally honest and I wasn't making fun of his lifestyle or anything, and I got letters from gay people saying thanks for asking the question. To me, that was something people would honestly like to know the answer to.' His honesty shined when novelist Jackie Collins appeared on the show. Off camera he told her that he couldn't stand her style of sex-driven potboilers but he was more than willing to help her plug her latest.

The *Tonight Show* reached a low point with a special live from the set of *Cheers* after the cast had finished shooting the final-ever episode of the series. Waiting all evening to begin the broadcast they spent their time drinking and by the time Leno got to talk to them most were extremely tipsy. The show was a complete flop and Leno compounded the problem by criticizing them in a newspaper interview, although he claimed his remarks were off the record. It was recognized that Leno had no trouble with the monologue and stand-up but when it came to sketch-style comedy things went wrong. He seemed to be rushed in the interviews as well. Leno had a short attention span and it showed when he launched into his guests with a stream of questions, flying so fast he barely stopped to enlarge on their answers.

August was fast approaching and the lines were now being drawn for the heavyweight chat-show title of America in what would be known as The Battle For Late Night. Leno and Letterman faced eached other head to head in an unprecedented confrontation at 11.30. Leno looked forward to it: 'It's very exciting. Let the games begin. I think this is great fun. I think late night is suddenly the most exciting part of television. Twenty years ago it was eight o'clock and nine o'clock and the sitcoms. Now I think it's exciting. This is live television. It's happening live at CBS, it's happening live on the *Tonight Show*. It's happening live in syndication. It's happening live on Fox. I think it's great. It's millionaires arguing at late-night, battling for audiences. I just love it. It's hysterical.' As Letterman forged ahead in the battle Leno could see history repeating itself. Letterman had been the first to break into television and now he was leading the field once more despite not getting the cherished Carson seat.

> *Changing things in late-night TV takes time, like turning the Titanic around.*
>
> Jay Leno

Leno buckled down and by 1994 his fortunes began to change. With the appointment of a head writer the comedy ante was upped. He regularly delivered twenty jokes in the monologue on the issues of the day where Letterman would be more sparing. Most of Letterman's comedy came from stunts. Leno again concentrated on comedy writing. A week in New York had seen the *Tonight Show* being broadcast from a small studio. Leno was right up close to the audience and he discovered a spark that had long been lost from playing in small clubs. Returning to Los Angeles he ordered the set redesigned in a successful attempt to exorcise the ghost of Carson. With the demise of CBS in certain TV markets and NBC's run of hit shows, things began to change. When *ER* was launched on many stations at 10 p.m. it ran straight into local news and from there on to the *Tonight Show*. Leno began winning in Los Angeles and Chicago and even some weeks on the Letterman home turf of New York.

By the end of 1995 Leno had almost turned things completely around with the *Tonight Show* back in pole position where it had

decades. Leno put a lot of his renewed success down to
ew with Hugh Grant shortly after the news broke of
vith hooker Divine Brown. Leno opened up with the
ɔst of the world was dying to ask, 'What the hell were
ɣ?' Audience levels went through the roof that night
ι   s convinced that many were returning to the *Tonight
Show* ̤ ̤ᵣ a long absence. Leno's decision to find comedy in the
O.J. Simpson murder trial also counted. Letterman adopted a
moral tone, reasoning that the vicious slaughter of two human
beings was not grounds for comedy. Leno added a lighter touch,
scoring a big hit with a dance troupe named after the trial judge,
the Dancing Itos.

Leno's pleasure at coming out on top after a tortuous few years
was undeniable: 'I don't want to make it Dave against me. It's
not a matter of that. It's a matter of when we started the show,
it wasn't very good. This has been a turning-point year. I've been
able to be loose. The first year I wasn't myself. Also, we were
perceived as the bad guy. A lot of people felt, wrongly or rightly,
that Dave got screwed out of this job. I knew I was gonna get beat
up for about two years, but it was incredible. Every day there
was some horrible story. But you keep your head down and do
the work.' NBC rewarded their star with a contract until 2000
and a salary almost matching Letterman's $14 million a year. In
1996 Leno remained comfortably ahead of Letterman.

RICKI LAKE

What Kind of Mother Are You? Stop Stripping and Get a Real Job!
I Have the Hots for a Co-worker
Mom, When My Boyfriend Gets Out of Jail I'm Taking Him Back

Ricki Lake Show topics

From the sophistication of the *Tonight Show* when it launched in 1950 to today the talk show has endlessly evolved. The *Ricki Lake Show* is the show that currently dominates daytime (after Oprah of course). Distilling everything from Donahue to Winfrey, its choice of subjects reflect the social climate of the mid-nineties. Shows have included 'Back Off Boys, I'm a Lesbian – You'll Never Have Me!'; 'Yeah, I'm Only 13, but I'm Going to Have a Baby!'; 'You Have No Friends and Today I'll Tell You Why!'; 'You Think it's Okay to Hit Me, but Today the Abuse Must Stop!'; 'Today I Nominate You the Worst Boyfriend in America!'. Subjects unthinkable for discussion even ten years ago are paraded across American TV screens as Ricki Lake orchestrates the proceedings to the shrill cries of 'Go Ricki!'

> *It's a constant challenge to remain interested.*
>
> Ricki Lake

Lake's life-story could be the subject of one of her shows.

Categorized as a 'funny fat girl' she found fame at the age of eighteen playing Divine's daughter in John Water's cult comedy film *Hairspray*. She swiftly moved to Hollywood and found work in a variety of films alongside a recurring role in the TV drama *China Beach*. Her career went into a nosedive when the show was cancelled and she lost her home. Reduced to appearing in cheap straight-to-video flicks she decided to lose 100 pounds in weight and auditioned as a chat-show host. Her personality and interaction with the audience sparked immediately. The show became a mega-hit across daytime America thanks to the host and not least the on-the-edge subjects tackled. Sparks regularly fly across the studio in debates like 'Woman vs. Woman: Ricki, Please Help Us Settle Our Neighbourhood Catfight' but Lake's easygoing style helps bring some sanity to debates which often border on the riotous.

When the show first aired in 1993 it attracted a slew of imitators. Nearly two dozen shows appeared re-enacting the Lake formula and the same sensationalist topics. The vital ingredient they lacked was Lake's personality and eye-rolling attitude which appealed to viewers. Many were called but few were chosen. Casualties included former *Partridge Show* star Danny Bonaduce and ex-*Cosby* kid Tempestt Bledsoe. Former Education Secretary William Bennett declared war on the shows, blasting them for 'cultural pollution' and asking advertisers to withdraw their support. The ratings however were case enough. Only the best could survive in such an overpopulated environment and in a few years most had disappeared. Danny Bonaduce summed up the genre when he said, 'I always felt strange asking people about their problems. It was like, why am I asking you this, and even stranger, why are you telling me?'

Alongside the current daytime survivors in the genre, such as Montel Williams and Jerry Springer, the *Ricki Lake Show* revolves around the ability to provoke confrontation. Confession-style shows have now given way to the ultimate in disunity with full-scale violence lurking just beneath the acceptable veneer of talk. The secrets exposed in the studio have become much darker and more intricate and the element of surprise has become pivotal. The hulking figures of security men have now become an essential in the highly charged studio atmosphere. Lake once brought on a young woman and her boyfriend who proceeded to break the news to her that he was the father of many children by different women. As the camera closed in on the woman's dissolving world Lake told her, 'We're rooting for you.' Producer Gail Steenberg explains the appeal: 'The idea of having somebody on stage telling their side of the story and having the other person behind the stage so that you can see the reaction as the other person is, like, dissing them, or doing something to them does so much for the energy of the show.'

The key to Ricki Lake is that her apparent sincerity comes up against some of the strangest people to have graced a television studio. The sincerity is mixed with equal amounts of light-hearted fun. Witness the show, 'Surprise, I Want You to Be the Father of My Baby'. The general set-up is that a young woman has come up with the idea of her best friend's boyfriend impregnating her. The studio audience goes bananas and when the commotion dies down Lake delivers the line, 'What kind of cockamamy idea is this. You want his sperm!' Her incredulity is laced with a knowing smile. 'There's an empowerment to doing the show, it's just manic. The audience all wants to say something. In the beginning, they're giving me a standing ovation, and by the end, they're all pissed at me that they didn't get their question asked. Beyond that, there's keeping the guests straight, making sure they don't talk on top of each other, getting the purpose of the show out, plus watching for the cues to go to a commercial break.' The show airs in over 200 markets in the US and is popular with advertisers as it grabs the most prized daytime viewers, the 18–34 year olds. Although running second to *Oprah* in the US the show is often the winner here on Channel 4.

Lake is more than happy with her situation but has some reservations: 'I really like what I do, talking to the 200 people who come in every day, who genuinely care about me. But it's not what I imagined myself doing when I was a kid. I've done a lot of these shows three times now. We've done my boyfriend is cheating on me in twenty different ways. So it's a constant challenge to remain interested nine months a year and two or three shows a day.' Although aimed strictly at the limited viewing capabilities of a young audience the show aims not to go as far as some talk shows have done. Producer Gail Steinberg keeps to a strict code: 'There are lots of lines we don't cross. We have ethical rules. We have real stories, real guests, because young people are more comfortable with confrontation.' Lake is happier with the natural progression of the show: 'Yes, you see a lot of disturbing people on our stages. There are moments when I'm a little tweaked about stuff we do. I deal with people I wouldn't deal with in my everyday life. I don't know if I'll ever get used to it. I would like to get to the point where people see us like they see Oprah. Lately we've been doing more upbeat, positive shows because we're under a microscope. We never went as far as a lot of these shows. A lot of the finger pointing was unfounded. But we're being extra careful. It's my intention to do more upbeat shows but in all honesty it's a mix.'

Lake is a phenomenon who has tapped into the *zeitgeist* of the MTV generation but has kept her feet firmly on the ground. Having returned to acting in the film *Mrs Winterbourne* she plans to retire from TV at the age of 32 to study architecture.

ENDPIECE

In recent years the media in Britain have been regularly passing the death sentence on the talk show every time a new contender hits the spotlight. Gaby Roslin suffered an onslaught of critical abuse when Channel 4 launched her show on Saturday nights in a brave attempt to create some of the glamour previously associated with the golden era of the seventies. The format remained the same as it had for the previous 46 years, host announced guest, greeted them on to the set and chatted. But this very simple idea was like a red rag to a bull with TV critics, who quickly filled their columns with laments for the glory days of Parkinson and Wogan (who had suffered their own share of abuse in the past).

But, much like the insect that crawls out of your suitcase when you return from foreign shores and resists all attempts at stamping it to death, the chat show will not die. You just can't kill it. British sitcoms are reguarly held up to ridicule against their American counterparts but that doesn't stop ITV continuing to produce *The Upper Hand* or the BBC persevering with *Last of the Summer Wine*. Now, in 1997, Jonathan Ross has returned to the fold after five years, hosting a talk show for London Weekend which has all the respectability of *The Frost Programme*, with four diverse guests each week discussing a topic of the day. Clive Anderson has crossed from the rarified world of Channel 4 to mainstream BBC where his own brand of subversive rudeness now encounters a much higher calibre of guests, albeit with his sharper barbs toned down. Carlton have launched *Thursday Night Live* which puts Richard Littlejohn and Nicky Campbell into a veritable powder-keg arena where an explosive topic will see a studio filled with audience members carrying vastly differing views of the issue in question. A recent show on child molesters unbelievably had an admitted paedophile taking part in the debate with no attempt to disguise his identity. This show, although not fully networked, comes closest to the shock tactics employed by the most outrageous of America's talk shows.

Parodies of chat shows are now more popular than ever in the wake of Dame Edna Everage. Steve Coogan delivered Alan Partridge and Caroline Aherne's Mrs Merton has made the vast leap from a niche audience on BBC2 to the mainstream of BBC1. The trick has been that many members of the audience (both at home and in the studio) and indeed a few of the guests are still uncertain if Mrs Merton really is a confused pensioner with an incisive line in wit or an accomplished comedienne. In the space of less than two years the character has expanded to national recognition with a series of ads for British Gas. In America, the *Larry Sanders Show* remains supreme in the field of parody. Garry Shandling's remarkable portrayal of the insecure host of a late-night chat show is often chilling in its accuracy. Its use of real guests and the format of videotape for the show scenes and film for offstage adds a remarkable dimension to the series. Likewise Paramount's *Nightstand* with Dick Dietrich parodies the tumultous world of the daytime talk show with unerring accuracy and must fool many viewers with its volatile guests. It's Mrs Merton in essence but with a more knowing audience.

In the US the talk show, like the sitcom, is never in danger of being written off by the critics. It's part of the American psyche. It's always there. Americans worship their TV stars, especially Oprah. Recently she has launched an on-air reading group for her viewers. One of her first texts for her pupils was *The Deep End of the Ocean* by Jaqueline Mitchard, a novel about the kidnapping of a young boy from a hotel lobby. The author, who had struggled to bring up her three children after her husband died of cancer, claimed the story had come to her in a dream. The book had sold reasonably well but after the Winfrey show the sales exploded. The title hit the top of the hardback fiction lists of the *New York Times*, the *Wall Street Journal* and *USA Today*, toppling such authors as Tom Clancy and Stephen King. Winfrey had become an avid reader during her lonely childhood and had promoted books on the show before but had never set out to re-educate her viewership in such a schoolmistress style. The response overwhelmed her and she admitted, 'We touched a chord we didn't know was there.'

The chat show has come a long way. From late-night banter with Broadway stars in the beginning, it has now, almost half a century on, through its biggest star, Oprah Winfrey, become an incentive for audiences to switch off television and take up reading again.

BIBLIOGRAPHY

Bad TV – The Very Best of the Very Worst, Craig Nelson, (Dell, New York, 1995)

The Best of Parkinson, Michael Parkinson (Pavilion/Michael Joseph, London, 1982)

Box of Delights – The Golden Years of Television, Hilary Kingsley and Geoff Tibballs (Papermac, London, 1989)

The Boxtree Book of TV Stars 1992, Anthony Hayward (Boxtree, London, 1992)

David Frost – A Biography, Willi Frischauer (Michael Joseph, London, 1972)

David Frost – An Autobiography (Part One – From Congregations to Audiences), David Frost (HarperCollins, London, 1993)

Eamonn Andrews – His Life, Gus Smith (WH Allen, London, 1988)

For Ever and Ever, Eamonn – The Public and Private Life of Eamonn Andrews, Eamonn and Grainne Andrews (Grafton, London, 1989)

From Fringe to Flying Circus, Roger Wilmut (Eyre Methuen, London, 1980)

Here's Johnny, Stephen Cox (Harmony, New York, 1992)

Hot Air – All Talk All the Time, Howard Kurtz (Times Books, New York, 1996)

In Good Company, Michael Aspel (Robson, London, 1989)

The Late Shift – Letterman, Leno & the Network Battle for the Night, Bill Carter (Hyperion, New York, 1994)

Let's Talk! – America's Favorite Talk Show Hosts, James Robert Parish (Pioneer, Las Vegas, 1993)

The Letterman Wit – His Life and Humor, Bill Adler (Carroll & Graf, New York, 1994)

Oprah Winfrey – The Real Story, George Mair (Aurum Press, London, 1995)

The Oxford Dictionary of Modern Quotations, ed. Tony Augarde (Oxford University Press, Oxford, 1991)

Radio Onederland – The Story of Radio One, Keith Skues (Landmark, Suffolk, 1968)

The Radio Times 1993 Yearbook (Ravette, London, 1993)

Television, Francis Wilson (Century, London, 1985)

The Television Barons, Jack Tinker (Quartet, London, 1980)

TV Unforgettables, Anthony and Deborah Hayward (Guinness, London, 1993)

Who's Who in Pop Radio, Peter Alex (New English Library, London, 1966)

Who's Who on Television, ed. by Eddie Pedder (ITV, London, 1985)

Wogan, Gus Smith (WH Allen, London, 1987)

The World of Jay Leno – His Life and Humor, Bill Adler & Bruce Cassidy (Birch Lane, New York, 1992)

INDEX

219 ♦